After the
Passion

the empty tomb is not the end of the story,
meditations from Easter to Pentecost

D1446576

GARY STANLEY

After the Passion: the empty tomb is not the end of the story
by Gary Stanley

After the Passion: the empty tomb is not the end of the story
ISBN

Table of Contents

Easter Afternoon: The Road to Emmaus

Easter Evening: Jesus' First Appearance to Disciples

Eight Days Later: Jesus' Second Appearance to Disciples

Road Trip to Galilee

Week in Jerusalem

Acknowledgements

For many years my wife and I spent Lent, the 40 days before Easter, reading Walter Wangerin's *Reliving the Passion*. Wangerin invites his readers to venture deep into the story, to taste and experience that unforgettable week leading up to Jesus' crucifixion. The ancients called this focused pondering *lectio divina*.[1]

Every year I read Wangerin's final chapter with a mixture of joy and sadness as Mary Magdalene abandons her rage when she realizes Jesus has risen, and says to Peter -

Peter, are you listening? Do you understand? He is risen!

I didn't scream, . . .

[A]nd I'll tell you why I didn't scream. Because I couldn't even breathe . . .

It's a killing terror, isn't it? Exquisite and sharp—a painful, impossible joy.

(Reliving the Passion, page 155)

---

[1]   See *A Few Words About Lectio Divina*, in the back of the book.

Yes, Mary, that's exactly what it is—a painful, impossible joy! It leaves me unsettled, in need of more. I long to head to Galilee with Peter and Mary and the others to see the risen Christ, because He doesn't leave right away. He sets aside another 40 days to say goodbye, and I don't want to miss a single moment.

My poor pen will not do justice to the days following the Passion as Wangerin's surely would. But I couldn't let another year go by without delving into this 40-day journey Jesus takes with His followers.

The content in this little book has had several incarnations. It began life as a series of personal, daily reflections from Easter to Pentecost. It languished for a year or two formatted as a pdf begging to be downloaded. The time had come to wrap a book cover around it and put it in an accessible form.

All along the way, a gracious band of editors have corrected my spelling, tightened up my thoughts, challenged my assumptions, and encouraged me to cross the literary finish line.

So to my dear friends Alan Scholes, Leif Bilen, Don Rueter, and Dawn Geiger—many thanks, this is a better book, and I am a better man, for all of your attention. And of course to Luci, who has influenced the shape and course of all that I've written and become since our "I dos," thank you one and all! I'm looking forward to our next joint adventure.

Any mistakes, grammatical or theological, are mine alone.

Were not our hearts burning within us while He was speaking to us on the road, while He was explaining the Scriptures to us?

Luke 24:32

Introduction

The Gospel is story. And the Author of life uses story to show us who we are, what is going on, and why it matters.

After Jesus rose from the dead He very intentionally wove the individual stories of His disciples with His own story. For forty days, Jesus took them back through what had happened during their time together. He reminded them of what He'd said, revisited the key places and events, removed crippling doubts, repaired broken relationships, and gave them a new purpose for living.

Every morning for the 50 days from Easter to Pentecost, I invite you to spend a few minutes with me in the resurrection narrative. We'll listen around the edges of what is actually written and step *into* the story. One of my favorite ways to do that is called *lectio divina*[2] a suspicious sounding Latin phrase, fraught with danger, full of promise, and spiritually invigorating.

---

[2] If you want to "take the wheel" and not just "hitchhike" on my insights and discoveries during our journey, I suggest you read *A Few Words About Lectio Divina* located at the back of this book.

Our journey begins at not one, but two empty tombs. We will quickly backtrack to the three days between Jesus' death and resurrection for a grueling week, as we listen to Jesus' enemies plot and scheme in their unbelief, and face our own susceptibility to those same fatal flaws. Then we will linger for almost three weeks on the events and encounters of that first resurrection day. We will spend another week with Peter unpacking his fateful fishing trip at the Sea of Tiberias. Finally, we will climb the mountain in Galilee to hear Jesus commission His followers, traveling back to Bethany for a final goodbye with Jesus, and return to Jerusalem to celebrate Pentecost.

DAY

1

STEPPING INTO
THE STORY

*Now in the place where He was crucified there
was a garden, and in the garden a new tomb
in which no one had yet been laid.*

John 19:41

In 2004, The Passion of the Christ was released. Subtitled, theologically controversial, and ruthlessly violent—who would watch it? The reviews were mixed but the audience was not. It became one of the most watched films of all time.

But why?

Perhaps we encountered something far more engaging than just another telling of the Easter story. Our imaginations were stirred, our hearts were opened, and we experienced the exquisitely painful, piercingly wonderful joy of the Cross, and the Heart behind it all—we were invited *into* the story.

As the credits rolled after the movie, I could barely breathe. The final scene still replays in my mind as we are taken to the garden tomb:

Morning light pours into the tomb.

The empty grave clothes collapse in on themselves,

the outline of His profile.

Jesus slowly opens His eyes.

He stands—

His body travels past the fixed lens of the camera.

First His shoulder,

then His arm,

and finally the outside of His hand

comes into view.

I can see through the jagged hole

where the nail had been

and glance His thigh.

And then, awakened from some distant land,

I am overwhelmed by painful impossible joy.

In the theater that night no one around me moved. No collecting of coats. No making for the exit. We savored that singular moment when mortality was swallowed by immortality.

The movie credits finished their scroll and faded to black. The house lights came up and the audience finally began to make its way to the exits. But this time, in my memory of that night, one thing changed—my imagination awoke.

The screen flickers back to life. A robed figure steps into the foreground. It is Him! Jesus looks straight into the camera and announces, "There's more! Come back!

The story isn't over!"

No quick goodbyes. This is the Director's uncut version! This time the rest of the story won't end up on the cutting room floor. Jesus spent 40 more days on the earth. He's up to something and we're not leaving until we find out what it is.

DAY

{ 2 }

AFTER THE SABBATH

Now after the Sabbath, as it began to dawn
toward the first day of the week.

Matthew 28:1

Another sunrise brightens the sky. We're still in *chronological* time—that linear, measurable time that flows predictably down through the ages—the dawn of a new week. *Chronos* time infects our thinking, our perceptions, dictates our fate.

Chronos time doesn't empty a tomb. Nail wounds don't turn into scars over night. And the dead stay put if *chronos* has any say in the matter. That's the way it has always been— tick tock thinking.

But *chronos* isn't the only kind of time worth considering. *Chronos* is susceptible to another kind of time altogether. The ancients called it *kairos* time.

"In the fullness of time."
"At the proper time."

"At the right time."

This is God-time.

Not long ago ("the Passover was at hand") Mary and Martha were wearing the blinders of *chronos* time. Their brother Lazarus had died. Jesus arrived too late. It is now four days after the fact. Lazarus is dead and buried.

Mary sits and ponders. Martha paces while her thoughts run ahead. The past few days have brought them to the same frustrating place. They pick their words of faith and accusation carefully—the exact same words—

"Lord, if You had been here, my brother would not have died." Jesus, You're too late. You didn't come in time. You missed the moment. No one can turn back the clock.

"Your brother shall rise again."

"I know our brother will be raised on the last day."

No Martha, you don't know. Stop living in the moment and live in Me. Don't shove all of your hopes into some distant future. Place them in Me. "I AM the Resurrection."

"Yes, Lord; I believe that You are the Christ." But I have no idea what to do with that knowledge.

"Where have you laid him?"

That's more like it. Join us in our sorrow. Let it be. Play the dirge and mourn. "Come and see."

"Remove the stone."

"By this time there will be a stench." This is just going to make matters worse. Why add the smell of death to our pain.

"There is an appointed time for everything."

"Lazarus, come forth!"

Jesus, a handful of days before Your own death, You pulled back the curtain and gave us a glimpse of how the story ends. It is going to be all right! What looks like a tragedy isn't that at all. This is going to be a funeral with party clothes.

The events surrounding Lazarus' death were a rehearsal for something far greater. The question, "Where have they laid him?" will shortly be asked again but this time it won't be Lazarus we're looking for. The invitation to "Come and see" will be repeated in the near future and freedom will come forth from the confines of a forgetful, time-bound faith.

"I AM the Resurrection."

Yes, Lord; I believe you are the Christ too. But I believe in an abstract sort of way. I self-protect. I hold my breath. I defer hope against the possibility that I'll be disappointed. The delays manufactured by *chronos* wither a faith that holds its breath.

"Come and see."

Ancient of Days,

You always show up unexpectedly at just the right time. That's much of my problem—my expectations don't match Yours. Help me live in this season; wide-awake to the *kairos* moments You have waiting for me.

Amen

DAY

3

BACK ROOM CONVERSATIONS

Now on the next day, which is the one after the preparation, the chief priests and the Pharisees gathered together with Pilate, and said, "Sir, we remember that when He was still alive that deceiver said, 'After three days I am to rise again.' Therefore give orders for the grave to be made secure until the third day, lest the disciples come and steal Him away and say to the people, 'He has risen from the dead,' and the last deception will be worse than the first."

Matthew 27:62-64

It is Saturday; the resurrection is still a day away. Our side is muted in grief and fear. The other side is agitated and talkative. Easter will have to wait a bit longer as old rumors give way to new realities in the minds of Jesus' enemies. That "deceiver" said he would rise from the dead after three days.

Odd they got that mostly right. During the trial no one could seem to agree. The false witnesses couldn't get their stories straight. He said he would destroy the Temple and build it again in three days." No, he said he could destroy it. Yet now, one day later the danger may be even greater—if his disciples steal the body the last deception will be worse than the first.

Caiaphas, are you beginning to doubt what you knew for sure? Did you wake up with this new danger plaguing your Sabbath ritual? Did you discuss it with some of your Sadducee cronies, only to discover that you all awoke with the same dread thought?—*If I were one of his followers, I'd steal the body just to stick it to the leaders!*

Are you really trying to protect the people from a false messiah? Or is it something else? Is your heart so full of deceit that you can't help but project it onto others?

You must be consumed by your fears. What else could make you go back to Pilate again? He has already washed his hands of your charade. Push him too far and you just might end up on a Roman cross yourself!

Where does it end? More soldiers to guard the tomb, more thuggery to justify your judicious actions—more bribes, more paranoia? It is a dangerous game you're playing. You're making it up as you go now, bending ancient laws, inventing new ones—there's a word for this, "lawlessness." Careful Caiaphas, remember Jesus' words, "because lawlessness is increased, most people's love will grow cold." Feeling a bit chilly?

How could we, Christ's followers, have forgotten His promise to rise in three days? He said it often enough. Caiaphas remembered and tried to stop it. But it is so easy to forget His promises and stay frozen in fear.

Dear Jesus,

In this moment before heading into Your 40-day goodbye, help us remember this—You always keep Your word.

Amen

DAY

4

PIMPING PILATE

Pilate said to them, "You have a guard; go, make it as secure as you know how." And they went and made the grave secure, and along with the guard they set a seal on the stone.

Matthew 27:65-66

The creation is holding its collective breath. The body is in the tomb. The rock has been rolled into place. No one gets in or out. That's the plan. Saturday is winding its way towards dusk. It's a day of rest—for some.

A little unfinished business with the Roman authorities, hey Caiaphas?

Pilate, we need to put an official seal on this business.

One thing leads to another, doesn't it? Pilate tolerates your presence, nothing more. You can hear it in his tone.

You have a guard. Go.

No chitchat. No, "Well that was quite an eventful day, wasn't it Caiaphas!" No, "Didn't expect to see you today! It is a bit further than a Sabbath walk between our houses, I would have thought! Still, what's a little breaking the Sabbath between friends?"

Everything is strictly business. There's a cover-up going on that needs more cover.

Pilate is worried too. His wife had that troubling dream about Jesus. She warned him to have nothing to do with Jesus (Matthew 27:19). Pilate tried to have it both ways, washing his hands as he handed down a guilty verdict. He woke with a nagging thought, "I should have listened to her. Here are Caiaphas and his cronies, trying to get me to do some more of their dirty work."

Caiaphas, you can read it all in Pilate's eyes. Don't push him too far. He could go either way. Keep bowing; feed his ego so it doesn't devour you. You are both political creatures not religious ones. Take what you can get.

Pilate doesn't fold; he keeps his cards and his options close to his chest. But he doesn't raise either—

You have a guard. Go make the tomb secure.

Only Jesus' enemies seem to be talking today. We don't hear one word from the side of those who love Jesus—what is there to say?

Plenty.

Light of the World,

Why do I doubt in the dark what was so clearly taught in the light? What am I missing? Oh! Now I see. I can't help but walk in the dark when I walk alone. What I'm missing is You, the Light of the World.

Amen

DAY

5

BAD DAY FOR CAIAPHAS

*Now while they were on their way, behold, some
of the guard came into the city and reported to
the chief priests all that had happened.*

Matthew 28:11

Every conversation has a backstory. It doesn't matter if you're
a woman, an angel, or a Roman guard. The words spoken
and heard on that first Easter morning have a context larger
than the moment. The soldiers' report to the chief priests
and Caiaphas is a case in point.

Poor Caiaphas! Another early morning for you. You're not
getting much sleep these days. What did you think when
you first heard the news? How did the guards break it
to you?

"Ah, good morning, Sir. Well, actually 'good' probably
won't work this morning. Thing is, ah, how to put it? You
know all this business about Jesus rising from the dead in
three days? Wait, of course you know. You're the one who
asked Pilate for a guard to secure His tomb. The thing is,

well, can I ask you a question? Have you ever considered the possibility—I know this is going to be a stretch, but is it possible that this Jesus knew what he was talking about? . . . Why do I ask? Actually, this could end up being one of those really funny stories once we get past the immediate embarrassment of the thing."

Caiaphas, the guards must have thought you'd react better than Pilate. Which power will they submit themselves to? Pilate would have had them executed in short order. You're more into hush money, fabrication, and denial, aren't you?

They say power corrupts—guess it depends on the kind of power we're talking about. You don't believe in resurrection power and that's the back conversation that pollutes your world and blinds you to the truth.

Truth and Life,

What don't I believe about You that keeps me deaf, dumb, and blind to Your voice? How much evidence to the contrary will it take before my first impulse is to trust You and not self-protect? Please, I don't want to be one of the willfully blind—open my eyes and my heart.

Amen

DAY

❧{ 6 }❧

RIGOR MORTIS OF BELIEF

They will not be persuaded even if someone rises from the dead.

Luke 16:31

The conspiracy is fraying around the edges, Caiaphas. If you and Pilate had left the tomb alone perhaps your future lie about the disciples stealing the body might have sounded plausible. But you didn't do that, did you? Can't get off the merry-go-round, can you? Everything you do now accomplishes the exact opposite of what you intended.

You're fighting gravity, Caiaphas. Do you think you can bribe your way out of this anymore than you can bribe your way into heaven? Oh wait, you're a Sadducee! You don't believe in the resurrection from the dead. Never have, never will—no matter what.

Reminds me of Jesus' parable about Lazarus and the rich man in Luke Chapter 16.

"I'm in torment," says the rich man—from his spot in hell. "Send Lazarus back from the grave to tell my brothers so they can escape my fate."

"Wouldn't work," replies Father Abraham. "Even if someone came back from the dead they still wouldn't believe"—no matter what.

Jesus could have been talking about you, Caiaphas. Perhaps He was. But this rigor mortis of belief didn't just happen, did it? No, it started earlier, and the backstory will be worth another visit tomorrow.

Author and Perfecter of Faith,

My life is full of old conversations, some good and some bad. Tune my ear to the truth. Edit the tapes that run in the background of my thought. Sift my life of old habits and beliefs that pollute my faith. I trust You more than I do the old canard: "It is best to leave well enough alone."

I long for more.

Amen

DAY

7

THE COVER UP

Now while they were on their way, behold, some of the guard came into the city and reported to the chief priests all that had happened. And when they had assembled with the elders and counseled together, they gave a large sum of money to the soldiers, and said, "You are to say, 'His disciples came by night and stole Him away while we were asleep.'"

Matthew 28:11-13

Caiaphas, once you adopt a strategy you certainly stick with it. Invent a lie, circle the wagons, and bribe someone to promote the lie. You've moved way beyond the 30 pieces of silver you offered Judas. We're now talking about a "large sum of money." When you've repeatedly confirmed you hold a losing hand it is time to stop betting—only you can't. You keep wagering more in the false hope that you can win back your losses.

The Book of Acts preserves the irony of your stubborn, self-imposed blinders with your final recorded words.

"What shall we do with these men (Peter and John)? For the fact that a noteworthy miracle has taken place through them is apparent to all who live in Jerusalem, and we cannot deny it. But in order that it may not spread any further among the people, let us warn them to speak no more to any man in this name." (Acts 4:16-17)

You continued down the same dead-end road until you too were removed by the same Vitellius that orchestrated Pilate's fall from grace three years earlier. And the ironies don't stop there.

At the end of December, 1990, one of the most significant New Testament-related archaeological discoveries ever made came to light in Jerusalem: the tomb of Caiaphas, high priest in Jerusalem at the time of Jesus' death. Some of the ossuaries found in the tomb were inscribed with the name "Caiaphas," the most magnificently decorated of them was inscribed with the name "Joseph bar Caiaphas."[3]

Even now your attempts to cover things up (down to your own grave!) have a way of confirming the historical accuracy of the very thing you hoped to conceal.

---

[3] "To Bury Caiaphas, Not to Praise Him," by David Flusser, member of the Jerusalem School, January 1, 2004.

Dear Jesus,

I long for the day when You will pull back the curtain and everything will be revealed. But in the dark corners of my soul I still sense that old fear of "being found out"— exposed. I don't want to live a self-protected life. Rip away, Loving Ravager of my heart,

Amen

DAY

8

ECHOES, THE ULTIMATE SELF-TALK

"And if this should come to the governor's ears, we will win him over and keep you out of trouble." And they took the money and did as they had been instructed; and this story was widely spread among the Jews, and is to this day.

Matthew 28:14-15

There are competing stories afoot. Did a miracle take place, or just some mischief?

Jesus is only one day out of the grave and already lines are being drawn! Battle lines, storylines, lines of thought. Lines that can trip and tangle. Lines that trace the boundaries of the fortresses and prisons that defend and define us.

The ancients have a word for these boundaries, they call them *ochuromas,*[4] the strongholds, or houses of belief, that we construct from cradle to grave. They are the conclusions we have reached about ourselves, and all that surrounds us. Settled patterns of emotional, spiritual, intellectual beliefs that influence the competing stories we are likely to tell and trust.

Peel back this odd sounding Greek word, *ochuromas,* and you will find the source for our English word, *echo.* Echoes throw back our own words as if originating from another source.

The echo chambers on Easter morning ricochet from the empty tomb to the High Priest's headquarters. Wonder what was bouncing around in Caiaphas' head?

Miracles don't happen.

Never have.

Better that one man die

than a whole
nation parish.

That's not murder;

that's managing an
impossible situation.

---

4   "For the weapons of our warfare are not of the flesh, but divinely powerful for the destruction of *fortresses*". "We are destroying speculations and every lofty thing raised up against the knowledge of God, and we are taking every thought captive to the obedience of Christ" (II Corinthians 10:4-5).

Right and wrong are
subtle concepts.

      Yes, very subtle.

We are drawn to the version of the facts that casts us in the best light. The version we want to be true. Everyone thinks they are basically good and competent—even those on death row.

They are called strongholds for a reason.

Dear Truth and Way,

My heart is hard of hearing too. I catch so little of what You are saying in the midst of my own self-talk. I hate being so deaf to the wondrous strains that accompany Your presence. Filter out the soundtracks sung by the guiding fictions of this world and tune my heart to the music of Heaven.

Amen

YOU CAN'T HAVE IT BOTH WAYS

"And if this should come to the governor's ears, we will win him over and keep you out of trouble."

Matthew 28:14

"What I have written I have written."

John 19:22

Three days earlier, Pilate had reached the end of his patience. He had the inscription - "JESUS THE NAZARENE, THE KING OF THE JEWS" posted over Jesus' cross. It was common practice to publicly display the offense during executions.

The chief priest objected. Pilate's inscription made it sound as if Jesus actually was the King of the Jews. They wanted Pilate to change the wording. Pilate refused; "What I have written I have written."

Pilate was attempting to navigate between the proverbial rock and a hard place, and he can't find open water. Conspiracies are like that. One compromise leads to another, and one after that. Did the High Priest "win" him over? Hard to say.

Pilate played no further part in the biblical text. Yet history tells us that three years later, Pilate had one too many local "messiahs" killed, and Vitellius, the imperial legate of Syria, relieved Pilate of his post as governor and ordered his return to Rome. No one knows for sure what happened to Pilate after that. Except this –

Pilate continued to dance between a rock and a hard place. There's a medieval legend that he haunts parts of France and Switzerland causing demonic disturbances. Another legend from that area claims that Pilate's body rises from Lake Pilatus, every Good Friday. On the other hand, Tertullian, an early church father, wrote that Pilate was "a Christian in his conscience." The Greek Orthodox Church canonized his wife and the Ethiopian Church proclaims June 25th as St. Pilate's Day.[5]

Ah Pilate, I wonder where you ended up? You can't have it both ways in Eternity.

---

[5] "History of the Players" by Bill Petro, see petroslog.blogspot.com/2007/04/history-of-players.html

Healer of Divided Hearts,

I'm tired of trying to have it both ways—to live comfortably in this life and still live for the next. Hold my heart next to Yours and it won't be divided anymore.

Amen

DAY

✦{ 10 }✦

SLEEPWALKING INTO WIDE AWAKE

When the Sabbath was over, Mary Magdalene, and Mary the mother of James, and Salome, bought spices, so that they might come and anoint Him. Very early on the first day of the week, they came to the tomb when the sun had risen. They were saying to one another, "Who will roll away the stone for us from the entrance of the tomb?"

Mark 16:1–3

Mary, what woke you up so early this morning? Did you sleep at all? Bet you're bone-tired, cried-out and worn-down.

Glad you have the company of the other Mary and Salome. You brought spices to anoint His body but none of you really have a plan. Who will move the stone for you?

Your body is up and going through the motions but your mind and spirit aren't engaged. You're still trapped in the nightmare of the last three days, and sealing the tomb didn't bring you closure. You're not done with Jesus yet. You hope to reopen a few things—you haven't said "Goodbye."

Funny word, "goodbye." You can spell it with or without an "e" and with or without a hyphen. Because it isn't a word, it is a blessing and a prayer, a contraction of "God be with you." Same thing is true in most languages. This is about placing Jesus back in God's care, isn't it?

Oh Mary! You're sleepwalking right into the most wide-awake anyone can ever be. Because you are only a few steps from the most wide-awake Person there ever was.

It hurts so bad to be on the other side of a barrier blocking you from the one you love. That's why you came. To be close to Jesus even if you can't touch Him. But it would take a court order to open the tomb for you—or a miracle.

Mover of Stones,

I'm pretty sure that Mary misses You more than I do. When I'm bone-weary I'm far more likely to turn on the television, or engage in some mindless activity. But right now, in this moment, I really do miss You! And I don't need a stone rolled out of my way, I just need to come Home.

Amen

DAY

⚜ 11 ⚜

QUAKES AND GRAVES

And behold, a severe earthquake had occurred, for an angel of the Lord descended from heaven and came and rolled away the stone and sat on it. And his appearance was like lightning, and his clothing as white as snow. . . . The angel said to the women, "Do not be afraid; for I know that you are looking for Jesus who has been crucified. "He is not here, for He has risen, just as He said. Come, see the place where He was lying. Go quickly and tell His disciples that He has risen from the dead."

Matthew 28:2–3, 5–7

Things are starting to move again. This is the second earthquake in three days (Matthew 27:51). Invisible beings are visible. Heaven and earth are commingling, and more than the earth is being shaken.

In the midst of all this turmoil sits an angel!

Ladies, paint a picture for me. What did he look like sitting on that big slab of stone? Was he leaning back on locked elbows, with his robes spread out and his feet dangling off the edge? Did he have a smile on his face? How much could you make out in the radiant light of his presence? How close did you get?

I know all of you were terrified (Luke 24:5), and who could blame you! You fell on your faces, but you also listened and followed instructions.

Your collective obedience is humbling. I wonder if a group of men would have done the same?

You who ride the heavens on the back of angels, and thunder Your presence before Your enemies,[6]

Roll away the stones blocking me from You. And let me hear Your message again, I promise to listen and obey this time, with Your help.

Amen

---

[6]   Psalm 18:10

DAY
❧{ 12 }❧

UNEDITED TRUTH

Two men stood near them in dazzling clothing;
and as the women were terrified and bowed their
faces to the ground, the men said to them, "Why
do you seek the living One among the dead?"

Luke 24:4-5

Men or angels? One angel or two? Did the women enter the tomb before or after they saw the angel(s)? Mary, when did you meet Jesus, before or after fetching Peter? There are a host of unresolved questions surrounding the events of that first Easter morning.

Oddly enough there is no record that any of the disciples quizzed you or the other women about the discrepancies in your accounts. Watch any television detective worth his salt and you'd see him sorting out the smallest details. Of course, that's fiction. In the real world the unedited truth isn't so neatly packaged. If all of the eyewitness accounts fell into lockstep, there'd be far more suspicions of collusion, or a conspiracy—"let's get our stories straight before anyone asks."

There's another reason for the lack of detailed cross-examinations. Something that all of you had complete agreement on—Jesus is alive, just like He said. Makes everything else of secondary importance—or it should.

A lot of folks say, "I'll believe just as soon as I get all of my (secondary?) questions answered." Sounds like the same strategy Satan used back in the Garden of Eden. Bet he's still working that same dodge today.

God loves an honest questioner. But He doesn't jump through hoops, turn stones into bread, or jump off pinnacles just because someone insists on putting more conditions on the facts before granting belief.

There's always enough evidence for anyone open to belief, and never enough evidence for one who is closed to belief.

Lord of the Narrow Gate and the Needle's Eye,

I know Christianity is the thinking person's faith, but my head is getting in the way of my heart. Saving faith isn't a propositional truth, it is a personal truth; not adherence to a set of beliefs but allegiance to You. Why can't my heart remember? And why do I care more about tangential matters than about You? Help me, my heart is prone to wander.

Amen

DAY

❦ 13 ❧

EMPTY AND FULL OF QUESTIONS

Now on the first day of the week Mary Magdalene came early to the tomb, while it was still dark, and saw the stone already taken away from the tomb. So she ran and came to Simon Peter and to the other disciple whom Jesus loved, and said to them, "They have taken away the Lord out of the tomb, and we do not know where they have laid Him."

John 20:1-2

Mary, have you ever heard of *cognitive dissonance*? It's what happens to a person when their brain tries to hold two contradictory ideas at the same time, e.g. "Look before you leap," but "He who hesitates is lost."

What to do? What to believe? The dead tend to stay dead. But the tomb is empty, and angels are talking.

But you didn't wait to hear what the angels had to say, did you, Mary?

You jumped to a perfectly reasonable conclusion that completely missed the truth. If you had stayed with the other women, and listened to the angels (Mark 16:5-6), the empty tomb would not have been a source of angst but one of joy.

I can picture you running from the tomb back into the city. Better hurry and find Peter and John! You're going to need several more sets of eyes and ears on the events of this day before your heart stops racing and your mind stops jumping to conclusions.

Oh Mary, you're still in the most confusing part of the story. You will soon become the first evangelist—but not yet.

I've read ahead. The answers to all that you seek are back the way you came. Turn around, Mary! You are about to run into One Who will speak is a single word removing all of your uncertainty.

Dear Breath of Life,

I keep getting ahead of myself, just like Mary. I react before I have the whole story. Draw conclusions before I've listened to all of the evidence. My faith hyperventilates when it ought to hope. Oh Breath of Life, be a calming hand on my heart when I have no idea what's around the next corner.

Amen

DAY

14

WHAT'S IN A NAME?

Jesus said to her, "Woman, why are you weeping? Whom are you seeking?" Supposing Him to be the gardener, she said to Him, "Sir, if you have carried Him away, tell me where you have laid Him and I will take Him away." Jesus said to her, "Mary!"

John 20:15-16

Mary, you returned to the garden tomb with the same troubling anxiety you had when you left to find Peter. But this time a single word will unravel all of your cares.

"Mary!"

Your downcast eyes look up into His face at the sound of your name. There's not another word that could be spoken that so says it all.

Unspeakable joy floods your tears. It is Him! You start to blubber as you bury your face in the folds of His garment, completely undone and whole at the same time.

When You speak her name there in the garden it isn't a greeting, is it? It's an invitation, a calling, a passport that frees her to come. The one word that settles everything and removes all doubt.

Naming is a first order priority with You, the "Naming God." You name the stars, and everything under the stars. You first taught Adam to name everything in his domain. And You remind us that we all derive our name from You (Ephesians 3:15). Yet, each and every one of us still tries to make a name for ourselves. You'd think after the Tower of Babel (Genesis 11) we'd have learned not to do that. But we haven't. We continue to strive for labels when we could know what is truly inside the packaging from the One who made us.

And one more thing.

Mary, I see now that you know the most fundamental truth of naming—the one who names you is also your master. Let anything or anyone else name you and they own you.

No wonder we long to hear our name from Your lips! We don't know who we are any other way.

Dear Jesus,

Say my name, Jesus. I need reminding in these confusing times.

Amen

DAY

15

RABBONI

She turned and said to Him in Hebrew,
"Rabboni!"

John 20:16

Mary, the first thing out of your mouth in your startled
surprise is *Rabboni*.[7] Wonder if anyone else would find his
or her unedited heart offering such a response? Would your
friend Peter, the fisherman? Unlikely. Three days ago, he
was cussing like a sailor when cornered on the High Priest's
premises. The first thing out of his mouth when surprised
was more likely to be scatological than soteriological.[8]
There's still a lot of "Simon" in Peter.

But you, Mary, you hear your name and your heart leaps
through your lips with, *Master*! In that moment you knew
who you were, who He is, and the nature of your relationship.
What more is there? Your checkered, confusing past is,
well . . . past.

---

[7]   Aramaic for Master
[8]   matters of salvation

Help me out, Mary. I see your first encounter with Jesus like a rehearsal for my first taste of Heaven. Will I be distracted by the presence of angels, or friends and family? Will I miss my moment with Him? I'm scared, Mary. It is easy for my heart to picture Heaven full of wonders and loved ones and fail to anticipate what makes it Heaven in the first place—His presence.

Dear First and Last,

My imagination is captivated with tales of Paradise filled with wonders and rewards, but Your presence is often secondary or nonexistent. How can I mirror Mary's response when I'm far more captivated by secondary things like the ministry and accumulating knowledge than I am with You. Please, help me build my life around You instead of everything else—maybe then I too will find "Master" to be my first response in Heaven when I greet You.

Amen

DAY

16

CLINGING

Jesus said to her, "Stop clinging to Me, for I have not yet ascended to the Father."

John 20:17

Jesus, You always seem to bring everything back to the Father. Why is that?

The first thing out of your mouth at twelve years of age was, "I must be about My Father's business" (Luke 2:49). On the night of Your betrayal, You said that You are the only way to the Father (John 14:6). And You didn't stop there. You reminded them that You take all of Your instructions from the Father (John 5:19). And when all things are put in submission to You, You will turn right around and submit everything to the Father–including Yourself (I Corinthians 15:28).

You are on a mission from God the Father. Your submission to the Father in all things is crystal clear. But that goes against the spirit of the day. Submission smacks of slavery, repression, and inequality, not intimacy, equal value, and oneness.

Are You always going to be in submission to the Father? I think You are—I think it has never been any other way. In the Dance of the Trinity someone always leads, and I believe that role has always been the Father's.

But tell me Jesus, what is it about Mary clinging to You and Your mission for the Father that causes You to tell her to let go? "Clinging" seems such a needy desperate word. Can't tell from the text whether You immediately made her stop, or if You gave her a good long hug and then lovingly disentangled Yourself as You spoke. Either way, You clearly are not done with your assignment from the Father, and clinging isn't appropriate–yet.

Perhaps this isn't about Your personal space in the moment, but a future promise of intimacy where clinging is well and good and very much welcomed. Perhaps that's why there is a needy, unfulfilled ache in everyone's arms to hold and be held that no human arms seem to satisfy. We were made for an embrace yet to come, where "personal space" will sound like a silly notion from another time and place.

Source of All Comfort,

Hold me too.

Amen

DAY

❧ 17 ❧

THE DAY THEY RAN

Peter and the other disciple went forth, and they
were going to the tomb. The two were running
together; and the other disciple ran ahead faster
than Peter and came to the tomb first.

John 20:3-4

Things are speeding up. One runner has now ignited two
more. Mary Magdalene's breathless announcement that
Jesus' body is missing has given Peter and John enough fuel
to get them moving. And the starting line and finish line in
this race are the same place—the empty tomb.

Fight, flight, or freeze. These are the universal responses to
danger, and something very dangerous is happening here.
But there is another choice playing out here, isn't there?

I've heard that the unhealed feminine is susceptible to
frozen passivity, and the unhealed masculine is prone to
pointless activism. But that's not what's going on. They are
purposely running into Mystery. And the Mystery they seek
will soon find them.

The goal of the race always defines the runner.

I miss that truth all the time. I look around at the other runners and measure myself against them. But I have it on good authority that I must fix my eyes on the Author and Perfecter of faith. If I do that, I too will run with endurance and not be encumbered or entangled by the obstacles I encounter in myself and along the way (Hebrews 12:1).

Still, can't help but think that if I were running with Peter and John that Easter morning, I'd probably be more concerned about coming in third than the moment merits.

Dear Finish Line,

Why do I care so much about how I compare to the other runners? I'm pretty sure we aren't in competition or even on the same course. The goal really does define the runner, doesn't it? Yes, there is only one place to focus in this race—on You. It seems I still have a long way to go, and I need all of the encouragement I can get.

Amen

DAY

✦{ 18 }✦

SEEING IS NOT BELIEVING

. . . and stooping and looking in, he (John) saw the linen wrappings lying there; but he did not go in. And so Simon Peter also came, following him, and entered the tomb; and he saw the linen wrappings lying there, and the face-cloth which had been on His head, not lying with the linen wrappings, but rolled up in a place by itself. So the other disciple (John) who had first come to the tomb then also entered, and he saw and believed.

John 20:5-8

John, why didn't you believe when you first saw the empty tomb and the linen wrappings lying there? Maybe the bigger question is, why did a second look change your heart?

Did Peter's presence help you believe? Could you trust your eyes after Peter confirmed the same scene? Or did it just hit you all at once that Jesus was everything He said He was?

Help me out. Why was the scene you "saw" a second time enough for you? Would it have been enough for me?

Guess that's the thing about faith, it walks the road right along with reason but doesn't stop when reason has run out of gas, as it always does. But just like the story of His birth, there are a lot of parallel signs that invite us to venture further down this road -

Angels announce Jesus' birth and resurrection.

Women are the first to know about both events.

There's an enemy trying to stop both comings of Jesus at any cost.

Jesus was wrapped in similar linen cloth at His birth and burial.

Hmm! As the women prepared his body, did Mary reminisce out loud about the first time she wrapped the baby Jesus in swaddling cloth? It's such an odd detail to have been included in the Christmas story, unless it was a foreshadowing.

Funny how the smallest detail can become the tipping point to faith. Perhaps a second look at the wrappings galvanized everything up to that point. Is that when you believed, John? Is that when you knew that everything was happening just as it was written, down to the smallest detail?

Fabric of Faith,

Who are You? You scatter clues all along the way and wrap certainty in rags. I am undone at the thought of You, the Holy One of Heaven, swaddled in the garments of earth. My faith would unravel if not wrapped in Your robes of righteousness.

Thank You

DAY

19

"GET OUT OF TOWN!"

The angel said to the women, . . . "Go quickly and tell His disciples that He has risen from the dead; and behold, He is going ahead of you into Galilee, there you will see Him;"

Matthew 28:5,7

Then Jesus said to them, "Do not be afraid; go and take word to My brethren to leave for Galilee, and there they will see Me."

Matthew 28:10

The message straight out of the tomb couldn't be clearer— Jesus has risen from the dead, and everyone needs to get out of town.

The angel said it. and then You said it.

The flurry of activity and words is building.

But this isn't one of those, "grab your life vest, leave everything else behind, and head for the exits." Don't panic, but pack quickly. And get the word out.

I tend to lose the immediacy of Your words in the wonder of Your resurrection. Right now, the city is packed with Passover pilgrims, and Your followers are lost in the crowd. Very soon the political and religious upheaval surrounding news of Your resurrection will turn confrontational. But now is not the time for that.

Perhaps Your intent is that Your friends leave for Galilee with the rest of the out-of-towners. Galilee is home. Where better to meet and unpack all that needs to be unpacked before You return to the Father?

You've yet to encounter Peter, walk to Emmaus, or surprise everyone by appearing in their midst. That will all happen today. But tomorrow will likely be a travel day and they need to get moving. You will go on ahead and they will have time to walk out of their old assumptions and into Your story.

You're driving home the point that Your followers still live in two worlds—one full of miracles and resurrections, and the other packed with risky ventures and street smarts. They are heavenly citizens and resident aliens, and that won't change until You return at the end of the age.

Dear Appointment Maker,

I wonder how often Your will for me involves some geographical location? Can't help but feel that You make appointments with me in far away places, where I don't know the language and can't occupy myself with familiar distractions. Some of the sweetest times with You have been in places where I have little control. I'd like to abandon my comfort zone and embrace You, the ultimate Comforter.

Amen

DAY

20

SEVEN MILES OF BAD ROAD

And behold, two of them were going that very day to a village named Emmaus, which was about seven miles from Jerusalem. And they were talking with each other about all these things which had taken place.

Luke 24:13-14

Nothing like a long walk with a friend when you're packing a load of questions. Sometimes you just need to get out of town to sort things out -

"Okay Cleopas, let's run through it again. Jesus is for sure killed."

"That's right. And three days later the tomb is for sure empty."

"The women are claiming to have seen angels, who said something about Jesus having to suffer and rise again."

"Peter and John checked out the women's story for themselves and are now thinking it's probably true. Especially since some of the women are claiming to have seen Jesus in person."

"That pretty much sums it up."

"Could it possibly get any wilder?"

"Don't forget, the High Priest is claiming the disciples stole the body."

"I don't think we can sort this out on our own in seven miles, or 700 miles!"

"Me neither."

Keep walking Cleopas. Company is coming. And the One who will soon keep pace with you will soon have your hearts racing with the sweetest burn you've ever known!

Dear Constant Companion,

You were there all along; Cleopas and his buddy couldn't see You any better than I can, but that didn't change the facts. The ancients loved to affirm Your presence—"I am continually with You; You hold my right hand. You guide me with Your counsel, and afterward You will receive me to glory" (Psalm 73:23-24), an old promise in no danger of wearing out. Awaken my heart to Your presence and remind me that I don't have to figure out life on my own.

Amen

DAY

21

BREATHING LIFE INTO THE BEATITUDES

While they were talking and discussing, Jesus Himself approached and began traveling with them. But their eyes were prevented from recognizing Him. And He said to them, "What are these words that you are exchanging with one another as you are walking?" And they stood still, looking sad. One of them, named Cleopas, answered and said to Him, "Are You the only one visiting Jerusalem and unaware of the things which have happened here in these days?"

Luke 24:15–18

A handful of wispy clouds dot the sky. A breeze stirs the upper branches of a sycamore tree in contrast to the stillness of the air on the ground. Two sets of sandaled feet walk a dusty road when a third traveler joins them. Below the swish of a long homespun robe, the third man's feet are nail-scarred.

The first two men are still in conversation as they walk the common road. The stranger listens for a while and finally asks, "What are you two talking about?"

The question brings everything to a halt. The awful reality of what actually happened to Jesus pushes the wild speculations of Jesus coming back from the dead into the mental file called, "Who are we kidding?"

One simple question unravels their fledgling faith, and a new wave of sadness and loss makes a step in any direction seem pointless.

"Are you the only one visiting Jerusalem unaware of the things which have happened?" asks the first man. He turns to his traveling companion and shakes his head. How could anyone coming from the city not have heard about the mock trial and crucifixion of Jesus?

A faint smile forms on the lips of the stranger beneath the shadow of his hooded cloak.

Jesus, You're loving this, aren't You?—in disguise and waiting to be recognized. The old beatitudes are about to have new life breathed into them:

"Blessed are the poor in spirit, for the Kingdom of Heaven will be made known to them by the King Himself."

"Blessed are those who mourn, for they will walk alongside the Comforter Who brings joy from the depths of sorrow by His very presence."

"Blessed are those who hunger and thirst for righteousness, for they will break bread with the Bread of Life this very day."

You are the only one visiting Jerusalem that week who is fully aware of what happened! And You are about to connect the dots for these two men.

Dear Beginning and End,

I need Your blessing too. When I'm trapped inside a pesky subplot that promises a bad end, I miss the bigger, all is well, happy ending story with You. Lift my gaze beyond the horizon of my paltry faith to see the distant land that is my true Home.

Amen

DAY

22

LOOKING BACK, WALKING FORWARD

And He said to them, "O foolish men and slow of heart to believe in all that the prophets have spoken! Was it not necessary for the Christ to suffer these things and to enter into His glory?" Then beginning with Moses and with all the prophets, He explained to them the things concerning Himself in all the Scriptures.

Luke 24:25-27

Less than four days ago, You were telling the Disciples that You are the Way, the Truth, and the Life (John 14:6). And here You are walking alongside two troubled travelers explaining the truth of the Scriptures, igniting their lifeblood, and leading them along the way.

Never thought much about You being "the Way." In my mind I pictured a cross bridging a chasm with Your children walking over "the way" into the Father's presence. But the bridge analogy is too static. I have a different picture now.

You picked an intriguing word when You called yourself "the way"—hodos (ὁδός). It has the feel of a journey, not so much an event as it is a process. "Exodus" and "odometer" find their linguistic origins in hodos. You are the road!

You are so much more than a one-time event! You open the door, escort us through, and become our companion along the way. Like the two troubled travelers, I need a traveler's heart to undertake this journey of knowing You as "the Way," "the Truth," and "the Life."

I won't be the same person at the end of the road as I was at the beginning, will I?

Dear Journey,

The prospect of a road trip with You stirs old memories of adventures past and the promise of new ones to come. Remind me again that traveling with You will take me where I need to go and along the way I will become who I need to be.

Amen

DAY

23

GUESS WHO CAME TO DINNER?

But they urged Him, saying, "Stay with us, for it is getting toward evening, and the day is now nearly over." So He went in to stay with them. When He had reclined at the table with them, He took the bread and blessed it, and breaking it, He began giving it to them. Then their eyes were opened and they recognized Him.

Luke 24:29-31

What was it? Did they see the nail scars in Your hands? Sharing a meal with someone who has been crucified would definitely be eye-opening! Or was it something subtle, some slight mannerism of Yours that gave You away?

It's as if 1500 years of written history had been compressed into a single afternoon. You walked them through the Old Testament's progressive revelation of who You are.

Did you draw a parallel between the prophecy that You would "bruise the Serpent's head" (Genesis 3:15), and Your cross being driven into the rocky skull called Golgotha?

Did You tell them about wrestling with Jacob (Genesis 32), or quote Isaiah 53 to them which reads like an eyewitness account of Your crucifixion?

Did You decide to flesh out the answer to David's prayer, "teach me Your ways" (Psalm 25:4)? After all, You are the Way.

Maybe, just maybe, You finished Your day-long lesson by reminding them, as You blessed the dinner rolls—"This is My body broken for you."

Surely, this is the first Lord's Supper done in remembrance of You!

Dear Bread of Life,

Why are mealtimes so important to You? Food and faith seem to go together in Your Kingdom. I wonder what the conversations will be like at those other mealtimes You have planned in the future, like the Marriage Supper of the Lamb? (Revelation 19:9) Will You take that moment to rehearse for each of us how our romance with You unfolded? Will we finally be able to tell our own stories without distortion or gaps? Can hardly wait.

Amen

DAY

{24}

VANISHING ACT

. . . and He vanished from their sight. And they got up that very hour and returned to Jerusalem, and found gathered together the eleven . . . While they were telling these things, He Himself stood in their midst and said to them, "Peace be to you."

Luke 24:31–36

In the 33 years before this You've never just vanished. Oh, You've walked away. Sought solitude. Needed time alone. But this is new. Why vanish now? Why not stay the night, or just walk back to Jerusalem with them?

No wonder folks wondered if You were a ghost or a figment of their imagination! I would too. Before this You were a constant physical presence with them. Now You're not.

You said in the End Times You'd come like a "thief in the night" (I Thessalonians 5:2). Was this to be a sign of things to come? Are You in a hurry?

Perhaps I'm not asking the right question. Perhaps You are always present, and we don't have eyes to see. Your last promise was that You would always be with us (Matthew 28:20). Only from now on it will be in a different way.

Yes, this is part of the weaning process of transitioning us from one member of the Trinity to another—like the parent who steps out of their child's line of sight only to reappear. As children we fear abandonment because we lack *object permanence*. Over time we come to realize that physical absence and abandonment are not the same thing—we grow up.

The ancients called this sense of abandonment the "Dark Night of the Soul." They also saw it as a necessary part of their spiritual growth process. Maybe there is a better analogy for what You are doing. You are nurturing trust in us, and like an old film photo, it needs a darkroom if it is to develop properly.

Unseen Reality,

I'm just going to say it—I don't much like Your invisibility. Life can look pretty lonely and scary. It takes a lot of effort to dwell down and remember that You are always there, even in the dark times. Sometimes I picture You sitting in an empty chair, or right beside me, but I can never sustain the moment. This whole invisibility thing just makes me miss You more. I guess my object permanence is still under development. I long for the day when the unseen is more real than the seen.

It already is.

DAY

❧ 25 ❧

A PIECE OF FISH AND AN OPEN MIND

They gave Him a piece of a broiled fish; and He took it and ate it before them. . . . Then He opened their minds to understand the Scriptures.

Luke 24:42–43,45

Eating a piece of fish is not the first thing that comes to mind when considering reasons to believe You are the risen Christ. Seems a valid assumption that ghosts don't eat fish (or anything else). But it's just so—simple. These are complex times and, well, I was expecting a more complex proof than demonstrating Your digestive powers.

But that's not the way of belief, is it? A chain of logical assumptions or proofs isn't why we believe. It's more like a rope of good reasons. Each strand combines with other strands, and after a while we're compelled to believe from the sheer weight of evidence. And with belief comes understanding.

Wasn't it Augustine who observed, *No one can know anything until they believe something*? Sounds like another way of saying You open our minds to understand by first giving us the gift of belief."

John parades twenty-seven witnesses across the pages of his Gospel in the service of belief.[9] You treat each of those potential believers differently. Nathanael is only one question, asked and answered, away from belief (John 1:47-49); Nicodemus will have to chew on the spiritual birthing concepts for a long time before he believes (John 3:1-15; 19:39); the Woman at the Well will have to develop a different kind of thirst before she can believe (John 4:7-42); a blind man miraculously receiving his sight opens belief in some but not others (John 9); and even after the resurrection You will continue to personalize belief for each of us as we will soon see with Doubting Thomas (John 20:25). The turning points of faith are mysterious and personal.

Belief in Me is always personal.

Jesus,

I remember the moment I met You. I was just a boy. I needed a miracle. And so I waited each Sunday for an earthquake or a power outage—a sign that validated putting my trust in You. I told a wise man about my strategy, and he

---

[9]   But these have been written so that you may believe that Jesus is the Christ, the Son of God; and that believing you may have life in His name (John 20:31)

thought a miracle made sense given the importance of the decision. "What do you think about Jesus dying for us and being raised on the third day?" he asked. "I believe it really happened," I said. "Don't you think He would rather base His relationship with you on *that* miracle rather than an earthquake, or some other sign?" I realized in that moment that I already had my miracle!

Yes, I remember that moment too.

DAY

26

CHASING DOUBT

After that, He appeared in a different form to two of them while they were walking along on their way to the country. They went away and reported it to the others, but they did not believe them either.

Mark 16:12-13

Is faith always reluctant? Doubt first, trust later? We seem predisposed to doubt. I know I am. Even after I'm sure, I'm not so sure.

Oh, to live in certainty! To be able to ask, believe, and live without doubt. Surely that's the goal.

Of course, we're told to walk by faith and not sight (II Corinthians 5:7). Sight doesn't require faith because there's no doubt in sight—and also no trust.

Perhaps what I've been seeking is a life without faith! That's not good.

So, what is it about doubt that can make it good or bad? Doubt can quickly get in the way of faith. When doubt is allowed to rule, faith is clogged up. But faith seems to grow out of doubt. Certainty doesn't make room for faith—doubt does.

So maybe what I need is a flexible doubt that can yield to faith and trust after being awakened. No wonder these 40 days are full of doubt.

Doubt is not the substance of faith, but it is the scaffolding on which faith is built before doubt is torn down. How useless a bridge that can't rid itself of the temporary supports used during its construction. Both the bridge and its supports are needed for a time, but the point is to end up with just the bridge.

So, all this doubting lays the groundwork for faith—as long as I realize that faith is to be built for keeps and doubt isn't. It is okay to doubt; just don't try to live there.

Dear Risk Taker,

I do not begin to understand how You tolerate all the doubt in this world! If I were You, I would have done just what the disciples expected You to do—set up Your kingdom on earth right then and there (Acts 1:6). I would banish all doubt and bend every knee to my rule. But that's not Your way. Certainty robs us of choice, and the ability to choose You is a gift beyond price—thank You.

You're welcome.

DAY

❧{ 27 }❧

TWIN DOUBTS

But Thomas, one of the twelve, called Didymus, was not with them when Jesus came. So the other disciples were saying to him, "We have seen the Lord!" But he said to them, "Unless I see in His hands the imprint of the nails, and put my finger into the place of the nails, and put my hand into His side, I will not believe."

John 20:24,25

Years ago, the guys I hung out with all saw a silly TV movie called, "Evil Roy Slade." They loved it. They quoted it. They used it as a metaphor for life. I had not seen it.

No way to join in their common experience because it wasn't common to me—no VCRs, DVRs, or Netflix.

Life can be so unfair!

Thomas, you didn't miss the movie, you missed the Messiah! All of life was now reoriented around Jesus' resurrection for eleven minus one.

You're not used to being on the outside. Of all the disciples you are the only twin (Didymus). From birth, you are the only one in the group who has always had someone oriented to life the same as you.

No wonder you reacted as you did. You're not just an empiricist looking for concrete proof. You're frustrated by something you had no control over and little experience with. You don't have firsthand experience with the risen Christ, and everyone else does. So, you make a vow.

Vows are serious things to make. They can lock you into untenable positions. You've now set the conditions under which you will grant belief. Bet you wish you hadn't done that.

I wish I could say I'd never done that, but I can't.

Dear Unconditional Love,

The very conditions I place on life become the barriers blocking me from life. I'll believe in You, just as soon as You—answer all my questions, grant me justice, humble my enemies, remove my problems, meet my demands. Forgive me; strip me of the conditions I erect between me and You. I miss You more than my unmet expectations. I lay them down.

Amen

DAY

28

SAVING DOUBT

After eight days His disciples were again inside, and Thomas with them. Jesus came, the doors having been shut, and stood in their midst and said, "Peace be with you." Then He said to Thomas, "Reach here with your finger, and see My hands; and reach here your hand and put it into My side; and do not be unbelieving, but believing." Thomas answered and said to Him, "My Lord and my God!" Jesus said to him, "Because you have seen Me, have you believed? Blessed are they who did not see, and yet believed."

John 20:26-29

Thomas, you held onto your doubt for eight days and thereby guaranteed your nickname "Doubting Thomas" for life. What was it like during those eight days?

Did you try to argue the others out of their collective belief? Did you simply stay away? Surely you wanted to believe, but something held you back. It wasn't long before your public declaration of doubt began to define you. We are trapped by the conditions we insist on and the vows we make.

Bet those weren't the happiest of days for you. Everyone around you is caught up in wonder, and you feel honor-bound to hold on to your cynicism. Doubt can be depressing, can't it? You must have found yourself conflicted by the deepest longings of your heart and your need to justify the position you've staked out.

Ask anyone around you what were the longest, loneliest days of their lives, and they'd all point to the three days before Easter. But not you. No, you managed to stretch those three lonely days into eleven. Yet God took those extra days of unbelief and fashioned them into a lifelong faith that tradition says took you all the way to India. He wastes nothing—not even doubt.

You are no longer on the outside looking in. Thomas, now you *know* that Jesus is exactly who He claimed to be. But Jesus has one more parting gift for you—a missed blessing. Remember what He said?

"Blessed are they who did not see, and yet believed."

Is it possible that in missing that first encounter with the rest of the disciples, that you could have had a blessing unknown to the others?

Maybe you weren't left out at all! Maybe you were set apart for your very own blessing. At the very least, you could have avoided those eight frustrating days of doubt.

In matters of belief you can set your own conditions, or you can leave those to Jesus. I've tried the first, I highly recommend the second. But isn't it wonderful that Jesus continues to pursue us in either case?

Dear Jesus,

You didn't belittle or dismiss anyone's doubts before or after Your resurrection. But You do expect me to do something with my doubts—bring them to You.

Amen

DAY

29

DESIGNATED MEETING PLACE

"Don't be afraid; go and take word to My brethren to leave for Galilee, and there they will see Me."

Matthew 28:10

This is the third time Your friends have been told to meet You in Galilee. You told them right before Your arrest (Matthew 26:32). The angels at the empty tomb repeated Your instructions (Matthew 28:7). And here You are, personally reminding them to head for the designated meeting place in Galilee.

Galilee is over 60 miles from Jerusalem as the crow flies and double that on foot. It could be a week before everyone is able to rendezvous with You.

No doubt they thought You would now usher in Your kingdom and defeat Rome. They are ready to engage a hostile world, and You want them to take a long walk.

Life is going to be full of unexpected turns for those who follow You.

All of this reminds me of the time Joseph and Mary traveled a whole day down that exact same road. They were headed home after Passover, and they had gone a whole day's journey from Jerusalem before they discovered that You weren't with them (Luke 2:44). It took them three more days to find You at the ripe old age of twelve engaging the religious leaders at the Temple.

Wonder if that was the event that began the family practice of establishing a designated meeting place? Or was that the moment a heavenly family value intersected an earthly family value? "I must be about My Father's business," You said at twelve. Soon You will add, "and so must you."

You know our lives will be fraught with danger and disruption. That's why You insist that everyone knows about the designated meeting place where the family will gather after cataclysmic events have scattered them.

You want us to know that no matter what, we will all meet up again, count noses, compare notes, and celebrate that everyone is safe and sound.

Living without a designated meeting place would be fatally foolish, wouldn't it?

Comforter,

That eternity longing You placed in my heart (Ecclesiastes 3:11) is aching right now. I long for home and welcome. I usually keep that longing under wraps because I know in this life that I can never really return home. I'm a stranger in a strange land and that is frightening. But I will travel hopefully, for I believe You will be there at the end of the road.

Amen

DAY

30

UNSPOKEN WORDS

The Lord has really risen and has appeared to Simon.

Luke 24:34

Not one word is said about this first encounter between You and Simon Peter, other than that it happened. Peter looked into the tomb, "saw the linen wrappings, and then went home *marveling* at what had happened" (Luke 24:12). And sometime during the day You must have appeared to Peter.

What happened? What was said?

Guess not everything is for public consumption. Still, I wonder. What if I let my imagination walk with you on that day of days?

Marveling works up quite an appetite, doesn't it? No fast food options here. Peter, if you're hungry go home.

You haven't been home for days. Home seems normal and nothing normal has been going on. You wandered the haunts where you used to go with Jesus.

Eventually you sought out the other disciples. John knows what you did but he isn't the sort to tell. Did you tell them what happened the night you denied Jesus? No, not yet. You still have to work up to it, don't you?

Did you contemplate your own suicide before hearing that Judas hanged himself? You're enslaved by your own words and deeds. How will you escape? How will you ever live with yourself? And then, Mary brings impossibly good news—the tomb is empty, Jesus is alive! You see for yourself and marvel on your way home.

The streets are beginning to fill. There's still a large crowd in town from the Passover festivities. You could have sworn you caught a glimpse of Him as you turned the corner! You're on autopilot. Your sandals take you home with no conscious effort on your part.

There He is! Coming out of your front door. You both lock eyes and immediately you're back in the outer court of the High Priest when Jesus turned and looked at you before being led away by His captors. You can't hold His gaze, and you look away. The confusion in your heart is overwhelming.

When you look up again He's gone.

Stumbling toward your door you rest your hand on the latch. What will you find inside? Is He waiting there?

No. Only breakfast, laid out as if you were expected. And one more thing—an ancient scroll is opened and positioned beside your meal. Your eyes fall on the words, "All we like sheep have gone astray, each of us has turned to his own way; but the Lord has caused the iniquity of us all to fall on Him."

You weep for the second time in as many weeks. But this time the tears don't taste bitter.

DAY

❧{ 31 }❧

GOING FISHING

After these things Jesus manifested Himself again to the disciples at the Sea of Tiberias, and He manifested Himself in this way. Simon Peter, and Thomas called Didymus, and Nathanael of Cana in Galilee, and the sons of Zebedee, and two others of His disciples were together. Simon Peter said to them, "I am going fishing." They said to him, "We will also come with you." They went out and got into the boat; and that night they caught nothing.

John 21:1-3

Peter, your words have the flavor of one who's thinking about returning to his former life. "I'm going fishing," you announce; and six of your friends decide to come along.

James and John are old fishing buddies, but what about the others? Are you glad for their company? Do they know anything about fishing? Are they going to talk your ear off or just be in the way?

What are you hoping for out on the lake? Isn't the town of Tiberias where Jesus healed the sick and fed the five thousand (John 6:1-14)? And aren't you fishing in the same spot where Jesus walked on water (John 6:16-21)?

So much has happened! Bet you're still confused about the future and any role you might play.

You know things about yourself now that you didn't know a couple of weeks ago. You're not in control like you thought. You couldn't even control your tongue when it came to confessing Jesus on the night of His betrayal.

Does that awful, defining moment still haunt you there in the boat?

What are you sure of, Peter?

. . . Fishing?

And how is that going for you?

. . . Oh that's right! You fished all night and caught nothing?

Are you beginning to suspect that you will never be able to return to your old way of life?

Peter, it's about time to get out of the boat—again. And this time you won't be walking on water, you're hooked and don't even know it.

Jesus has a way of ruining us for ordinary life, doesn't He?

Sovereign,

The Gospel is the Wrecking Ball that blows up the minor fishing expeditions I plan in the pond of what I think I can control.

The Gospel is the Bridge Burner that severs me from ever returning to the lesser success of my former life.

You are all inand by Your grace, so am I.

Amen.

DAY

32

CASTING NETS

"Children, you do not have any fish, do you?"
They answered Him, "No." And He said to
them, "Cast the net on the right-hand side of the
boat and you will find a catch." So they cast, . .

John 21:4-6

You set the relationship with a single word--

Children.

You meet them where they are--

You do not have any fish, do you?

You take them where they've never been—

Cast the net on the right-hand side of the boat.

But I know better than to do what You say. I'm not a child!

I don't need someone else to tell me my misfortune!

And I certainly don't plan to follow nonsensical advice!

I am not foolish, helpless, or lazy. What I am is tired, frustrated, and finished with ministry. What I am is prideful.

Jesus, You've caught me at a bad time.

Child.

Oh to be a child again! Not to be in charge. To be shielded from the raw, adult concerns of life. To know I can run home and be held in loving arms when I skin my knee; that there's Someone bigger than me that cares and looks out for me.

It's not working, is it?

No. It's not working. I don't like whatever it is in me that makes me think I can solve all my problems with hyper-vigilance. I don't want to be General Manager of the Universe anymore.

Move in an opposite spirit.

Not live on a hook? Not let the world dictate the pace of my life? Not measure my life by –

"Get it right."

"Get it done."

"Get over it."

Do something absurd like tossing my nets over the right-hand side of a boat designed only for fishing off the left-hand side? Live my life outside the expectations that I and everyone else place on my life?

Exactly.

DAY

✦{ 33 }✦

WHAT A MESS!

So they cast, and then they were not able to haul it in because of the great number of fish. Therefore that disciple whom Jesus loved said to Peter, "It is the Lord." So when Simon Peter heard that it was the Lord, he put his outer garment on (for he was stripped for work), and threw himself into the sea. But the other disciples came in the little boat, for they were not far from the land, but about one hundred yards away, dragging the net full of fish.

John 21:6-8

Peter puts on his clothes before swimming to shore and the other disciples opt to drag a net full of fish alongside their boat as they head in. What a mess! A mess of fish and a mess of men.

Everyone wants to get to Jesus as quickly as possible, but their initial responses slow them down from doing precisely that.

Wonder if there's a lesson here? Wonder if we will ever get used to seeing Jesus?

Easy to think that Peter could have left his outer garment in the boat and picked it up later. Easy to think the disciples could have abandoned the fish all together. But Jesus is the reason for the catch, and Peter surely doesn't want to stand in front of Jesus half naked.

When do we abandon our treasures and protocols, and when should we bring them along?

Jesus, up to this point You have been coming to them. You found Mary in the garden. You walked up to the men on their way to Emmaus. You crashed the disciples' meeting that night. But this time You are waiting on shore. You didn't walk across the water to them. You waited for them to close the distance.

How hard was it for You to watch them tangled up in their own efforts to get to You? Did a few extra minutes matter at all?

Everyone is hungry for You, even if they don't know it. Has everyone figured out what to bring to the party? I want to say, "Just bring yourself." That's what I've been taught and always thought.

Now I wonder if it might be messier than that.

Dear Lover of My Soul,

How can You wait on the shore for me to choose You? I postpone my moments with You, tangled up in the lesser things I drag around. Your humility in waiting for me is only matched by Your extravagance in making free will possible at Calvary. I don't know what to do.

Just come! Baggage and all.

Here I am.

DAY

34

FISH BAKE

So when they got out on the land, they saw a charcoal fire already laid and fish placed on it, and bread. Jesus said to them, "Bring some of the fish which you have now caught." Simon Peter went up and drew the net to land, full of large fish, a hundred and fifty-three; and although there were so many, the net was not torn. Jesus said to them, "Come and have breakfast."

John 21:9-12

You always seem to be preparing meals for Your followers. This is the second time You've fed folks in this location (John 6:1-14). But it's the conversation around the meal that holds the lasting substance. What did You talk about? Were there any awkward silences? Peter was so anxious to get to You, but now he's over playing with the fishing nets. Maybe he thinks they need his immediate attention. Maybe Peter doesn't know what to do when he's in Your company. Maybe no one does.

"Come and have breakfast."

One of the most important conversations in Peter's life will happen after breakfast, but not now. Now the conversation turns to what?

I wonder . . .

. . . "Hey!" remarks John, "Remember a few years back when we fished all night and caught nothing?"

"You'll have to be more specific!" laughs James.

"Okay. The time Jesus commandeered Peter's boat as a floating pulpit." (Luke 5:4-9)

"Thought that's the one you had in mind," smiled James. "Seem to recall Peter getting some advice on fishing that time as well."

"Well, I wouldn't want to say Peter is more needy of fishing advice than most, but . .," says John as he winks at Peter.

"That's right. After Jesus finished teaching, He told Peter to put out for deep water and try one more time," recalls Thomas.

"How many fish did you catch that time?" asks Nathanael. "I heard that catch nearly swamped both boats and tore up the nets big time!"

"Don't think we ever got around to counting that catch," replies John.

"Too scared!" smirks James. "Peter ordered Jesus out of the boat after that happened!"

"A hundred and fifty-three," offers Peter.

"That's how many fish you caught the first time?" asks Nathanael.

"No, that's how many fish we have this time," replies Peter. "We didn't count fish the first time. Fishing didn't seem very important that day. In fact, we left everything, boats, nets, and that catch of fish to follow Jesus."

"Yeah, but if we left everything behind to follow Jesus then, why did we go fishing last night . . ? Ah, never mind," mumbles Thomas as everyone suddenly becomes engrossed with his breakfast.

Dear Table Talker,

Why is table fellowship so important to You? What is it about long conversations over a meal? You can't eat on the run if you have to catch, clean, and cook whatever you intend to eat.

You mean for life to slow down in the company of friends and food. You share yourself each time You share a meal. I talk with my mouth full, seldom make eye contact, and wonder if it's my turn to clean the dishes.

Help me to slow down, swallow, and open more than just my mouth at mealtime—open my heart to You and those with whom I break bread.

Amen

DAY

35

GETTING YOUR HEART BACK

So when they had finished breakfast, Jesus said to Simon Peter, "Simon, son of John, do you love Me more than these?" He said to Him, "Yes, Lord; You know that I love You." He said to him, "Tend My lambs." He said to him again a second time, "Simon, son of John, do you love Me?" He said to Him, "Yes, Lord; You know that I love You." He said to him, "Shepherd My sheep." He said to him the third time, "Simon, son of John, do you love Me?" Peter was grieved because He said to him the third time, "Do you love Me?" And he said to Him, "Lord, You know all things; You know that I love You." Jesus said to him, "Tend My sheep."

John 21:15–17

Peter's threefold denial a few weeks earlier went deeper than he could possibly have known. The damage done that awful night by his words wounded his heart—and Yours.

In Peter's denial, he cut himself off from Your blessing and his destiny.

You are Peter, and upon this rock I will build My church, and the gates of Hades shall not overpower it (Matt 16:19).

With that declaration You set Peter's identity and his destiny. But right now Peter feels more like a lump of defeated sand than a victorious rock. All of this needs to be rekindled at a heart level.

Do you love Me?

"You know I do."

Then tend My sheep.

But what about Your heart? Does the Son of Man have a heart that can be wounded too? I wonder if You're doing more than just ministering to Peter's heart. Are You also getting Your heart back?

Years ago, I wounded my wife's heart with my words. She wept. I repented. She forgave. But months later she mentioned she was forgiving me again for those words. It puzzled me, "I thought you'd already forgiven me?"

"Oh, I did forgive you," she said. "But as I'm getting access to more of my heart, I've discovered the wounding of your words went deeper than I realized back then. It is all part of getting my heart back," she smiled. "And I'm forgiving in a deeper place."

So, Jesus, is this just about Peter's heart, or does the Incarnate Son of God, the Man of Sorrows, have a heart that can be broken too?

The old "once and done" strategy in human relationships is better left at the bottom of the sea, isn't it?

Incarnate One,

I forget that You, the Creator God were also fully human— You still are. No one knows how heart-breakingly deep and emotionally painful Your sacrifice to completely identify with us truly is. I only know that my heart longs to completely identify with You; I'm not there yet, but that is my longing.

Amen

LOVING ON OUR OWN TERMS

So when they had finished breakfast, Jesus said to Simon Peter, "Simon, son of John, do you love Me more than these?" He said to Him, "Yes, Lord; You know that I love You." He said to him, "Tend My lambs." He said to him again a second time, "Simon, son of John, do you love Me?" He said to Him, "Yes, Lord; You know that I love You." He said to him, "Shepherd My sheep." He said to him the third time, "Simon, son of John, do you love Me?" Peter was grieved because He said to him the third time, "Do you love Me?" And he said to Him, "Lord, You know all things; You know that I love You." Jesus said to him, "Tend My sheep.

John 21:15-17

Jesus, You're digging. Each question peels back another layer of Peter's heart. You've made the core issue perfectly clear—Do you love Me?

Interesting.

You don't ask Peter to explain himself, say he's sorry, or repent. His denial put distance between his heart and Yours. And now You're closing the gap. You're getting uncomfortably close.

Troubling.

It was his love for You that got him in trouble in the first place! You know he loves You. He wanted to be courageous and confident. To be Your stalwart companion in the most dangerous parts of the story. Instead he discovered he is also part coward. And now he is unsure.

Shaken.

Jesus, he loved You the only way he knew. But it wasn't enough, was it? And never would be.

Every step along the way Peter's love for You has been shaped by his own words and perspective –

"Go away from me Lord, for I am a sinful man!" (Luke 5:8)

"God forbid it (when Jesus says He must die), Lord! This shall never happen to You." (Matthew 16:22)

"Lord, with You I am ready to go both to prison and to death!" (Luke 22:33)

Peter has loved You on his own terms.

Didn't work for Peter back then, and it won't work for me now. But it is so hard not to think that loving You flows from my own efforts to love.

Do you love Me?

You know I do.

But just like Peter, I love You on my own terms. What else is there?

Plenty.

Lover of My Soul,

There is one mystery as great as Your love for me—that You would want my love in return. You know I love You on my terms, help me to love You on Your terms.

Amen

DAY

37

TEND MY SHEEP

Jesus said to him, "Tend My sheep."

John 21:17

Peter signed on to be a "fisher of men." He understood that; he knows fishing. He knows how to apply his strength and expertise to fishing. He knows how to work hard. And that is how he has tried to love You.

But You wanted Peter to love You on Your terms.

When You ask Peter if he loves You more than "these," You're referring to the fishing nets, aren't You? What Peter knows and is familiar with—approaching life with You on his own terms.

But You tell him to "tend Your sheep." You are the Good Shepherd. Peter doesn't know sheep. He knows fish. He can't do this. What You're asking is completely foreign to him. He simply can't do it in his own strength.

Stuck on a hillside when he'd rather be in a boat on the water. Is this lover of the sea to become a land-locked creature?

This isn't going to be about what Peter can do for You, is it? This is going to be about what You can do in and through Peter.

But what about me? I'm much better at loving You on my own terms too!

Tend My sheep.

Undone.

Great Shepherd,

I'm pretty sure that loving You is going to be messy, smelly, and uncomfortable. I'm just starting to realize that one of the most direct way to love You is to love Your smelly, messy sheep, of whom I am one. My, my!

Amen

DAY

❦{ 38 }❧

GALLOWS GLORY

"Truly, truly, I say to you, when you were younger, you used to gird yourself and walk wherever you wished; but when you grow old, you will stretch out your hands and someone else will gird you, and bring you where you do not wish to go." Now this He said, signifying by what kind of death he would glorify God. And when He had spoken this, He said to him, "Follow Me!"

John 21:18-19

Jesus, You're scaring me. I thought with forgiveness given, blessing secured, and relationship restored, this conversation would turn into some kind of "happily ever after." But You're talking death, and a grizzly one at that!

Peter's physical life is going to come to a bad end. You tell him that when he is old he will lose his freedom and die a painful death. Did he really need to know that? Couldn't You have postponed the bad news for a while and let him live in the comfort of the moment?

I wonder what kind of end awaits me? Sometimes (I know it's wrong), but sometimes I still fear You will desert me in the end. That I will die alone with no resources and little comfort. It is an old lie birthed in the untimely death of my Dad. But You know that, and this conversation has awakened that old fear in me.

So, tell me Jesus, why? Why mark Peter's life with this? News like this can't go down easy. This is a defining moment, an all in, nothing-left, to-the-death moment.

Peter will follow You because he knows there is no Plan B (John 6:68). There is nowhere else to go. We've both foolishly, pridefully, and sincerely declared that we will die for You—and You take us at our word.

So what can Peter and I hold onto?

Only this–

Glorify Me.

Dear All In,

I'm reminded of that old Amy Carmichael poem –

Hast thou no scar?
No hidden scar on foot, or side, or hand?
I hear thee sung as mighty in the land;
I hear them hail thy bright, ascendant star.
Hast thou no scar?

Hast thou no wound?
Yet I was wounded by the archers; spent,
Leaned Me against a tree to die; and rent
By ravening beasts that compassed Me, I swooned.
Hast thou no wound?
No wound? No scar?
Yet, as the Master shall the servant be,
And pierced are the feet that follow Me.
But Thine are whole; can he have followed far
Who hast no wound or scar?

The canvas of my life is Yours.

DAY

❦{ 39 }❦

WHAT IS THAT TO YOU?

So Peter seeing him (John) said to Jesus, "Lord, and what about this man?" Jesus said to him, "If I want him to remain until I come, what is that to you? You follow Me!" Therefore this saying went out among the brethren that that disciple would not die; yet Jesus did not say to him that he would not die, but only, "If I want him to remain until I come, what is that to you?"

John 21:21-23

This isn't morbid curiosity on Peter's part. This is survival. Peter's angst is my own. He needs some kind of comparison with which to measure his lot in life.

Jesus just told him how he would die. His selective perception hasn't registered the outcome that his death will glorify God, or the immediate command to follow Jesus. He's still processing his own death—who can blame him?

Peter casts about for some common ground, sees his friend John, and in that moment he needs to know how John will die. He needs perspective on his own death. Pharisees aren't the only ones who measure themselves by themselves (II Corinthians 10:12).

Jesus, Your response sounds almost heartless. "What is that to you?" Here is Peter in the throes of his own mortality, and You seemingly toss it back in his face with the most extreme comparison You can think of—"Who knows? Maybe John won't die at all!"

But You're not heartless. You care deeply for Peter. Your words marked him (just as You intended) for a life that will bring an eternal weight of glory. You're driving home the point that often misses my heart—"Follow Me and the rest will take care of itself."

The sign over Dante's Hell reads, "Abandon All Hope, Ye Who Enter Here!" I wonder if Peter saw a sign over the entrance to Heaven at his death?

"Welcome Home! You have now left the land of the dying and entered the land of the living."

Risen One,

When did You know? You spoke about it often enough. But when did You come to grips with how You would die? Was it as a young boy seeing crucified Zealots by the side of the road? When You first studied Psalm 22, or

Isaiah 53 (Luke 22:37)? That last night in the Garden of Gethsemane (Mark 14:32)? Before the foundation of the world (Revelation 13:8)?

Maybe a better question is how did You come to grips with Your own death? Yes, I remember now. You *endured* the cross for the joy set before You (Hebrews 12:2); You *entrusted* Yourself to Your Heavenly Father (I Peter 2:23).

Is that what Peter needed to learn? Or maybe, just maybe, the better question isn't about Peter at all.

What is that to you?

You mean how well am I enduring or entrusting?

A much better question.

DAY

40

THE 500

After that He appeared to more than five hundred brethren at one time, most of whom remain until now, but some have fallen asleep.

I Corinthians 15:6

Jesus, You've spoken to and fed far larger crowds (Matthew 14:21). There was another gathering where it seems You healed everyone brought to You (Matthew 19:2). And those that climbed the hill to hear Your Sermon on the Mount—what an unforgettable moment that must have been (Matthew 5-7). To have been a part of any of those gatherings would be life-changing.

But the 500! Set apart from any other group that gathered around You. What was the occasion? I understand that they all saw and experienced You *after* Your resurrection at the same time and place—strong counter to the charge that Your followers were hallucinating.

But maybe there's more.

There is no hint of another miracle taking place at that meeting. It doesn't appear that you supernaturally fed them, or healed them, or breathed Your Spirit on them. So why is there such a bond between this 500-plus crowd? A bond so strong it seems they kept track of each other for the rest of their lives? You must have done something or *said* something that marked them.

I think I know what it was.

As the door was closing on Your earthly stay, did You choose this moment to give them their marching orders? Was this the moment when You gave them the Great Commission (Matthew 28:18-20) and charged them to go into all of the world and live out Your message of hope and deliverance? You were weaving the narrative threads of Your Story into an unbreakable bond. And future events would never be the same.

Perhaps.

History records a handful of times when a small group of people embraced a commission that ultimately changed the course of history.

The 300 Spartans at Thermopiles.
The 10,000 at the Battle of Agincourt.
The 189 who fought at the Alamo.
The 385 at the Battle of Little Round Top.

And then there are the 500. If I'm right, they were heroic not just in the moment, but over a lifetime. And they changed not just history, but eternity.

Dear Commander and Chief,

Thank You for the opportunity to be a part of something wonderfully momentous that really matters!

You're welcome.

DAY

❦{ 41 }❧

THE MOUNTAIN TO CLIMB

*But the eleven disciples proceeded to Galilee,
to the mountain which Jesus had designated.
When they saw Him, they worshiped Him;
but some were doubtful. And Jesus came up
and spoke to them, saying, "All authority has
been given to Me in heaven and on earth. "Go
therefore and make disciples of all the nations,
baptizing them in the name of the Father and
the Son and the Holy Spirit, teaching them to
observe all that I commanded you; and lo, I am
with you always, even to the end of the age."*

Matthew 28:16–20

Mountains are the exclamation marks to Your story. You
restarted the human race with Noah after the Flood on
top of *Mount Ararat* (Genesis 8:4); You took Abraham and
his son Isaac up *Mount Moriah* on that fateful day (Genesis
22:2); and You camped the entire nation of Israel at the base
of *Mount Sinai* when You gave Moses the Law (Exodus
19:2). The *Mount of Transfiguration* (Matthew 17:1), the
Mount of Olives (Luke 22:39); and *Mount Zion* (Micah 4:7)

all highlight important moments in Your interactions with us. This "designated mountain" is none of those, but we've been here before, haven't we?

I bet this is the mountain where You laid out the principles of Your Kingdom at the beginning of Your ministry. You want Your disciples to remember Your Sermon on the Mount—the Beatitudes, the Lord's Prayer, and cautions about practicing their righteousness before men (Matthew 5-7). You are taking them back to an old familiar place and filling it with new implications.

When they heard the Sermon of the Mount (Matthew 5-7) they thought it only applied to them, the chosen people of God. No doubt they contextualized everything You said to their own experiences of alms giving, prayer, fasting, and keeping the Law. But now You've expanded the classroom far beyond the borders of Israel with Your command to "Go!" The target audience has now become "all the nations."

They can't simply stay home and try to live out Your principles in familiar surroundings. The essence of Your Gospel cannot be contained, defined, or practiced solely within the context of any nation or culture's experience.

Your Gospel doesn't destroy cultures; it transforms them! Folks from every tribe, language, people and nation will gather around Your throne (Rev 5:9)—and *still* be recognizable in their ethnicity. This isn't about turning people into Christian Americans, Presbyterians, or Capitalists. This is to turn people to *You*.

There is nothing else like this, is there? This isn't "religion" at all; this is "relationship."

People are always asking if there are many ways to Heaven. The answer must be, "Yes! There are countless ways to God." But every path leading to You has at least two things in common—it passes through the cross and is forever tied to the empty tomb.

Dear Shepherd of Souls,

I'm still troubled by something my wife asked me years ago—"What would it look like if you tried to fulfill the Great Commission at the expense of the Great Commandment?"[10]

I remember.

I asked her to hand me a mirror so that I could give her an accurate description of the guilty party.

I know. Tragic, how many try to fulfill My Great Commission (Matthew 28:19-20) at the relational cost of keeping their hearts open to Me.

I find it easier to do things *for* You than it is to do things *with* You.

Which is why I ended the Sermon on the Mount the way I did. "On that day many will say to Me, 'Lord, Lord, did we not . . .

[10] "You shall love the Lord you God with all your heart, and with all your soul, and with all your mind." (Matthew 22:37).

do many mighty works in Your name?' And then will I declare to them, 'I never knew you." (Matthew 7:22-23 ESV)

This is a mountain too big for me to climb.

That is why I promised to be there every step of the way.

Thank You.

You're welcome.

DAY

❧{ 42 }❧

OPPORTUNE TIMES

Then He appeared to James

I Corinthians 15:7

Little Brother James, why are you still here? The 500 have said their goodbyes and left. But not you. Are you listening to the echo of other words spoken on this very spot? "Blessed are the poor." "Blessed are those who mourn." "Blessed are the peacemakers."

Did you linger on the outskirts of the crowd like you did the day Jesus delivered His Sermon on the Mount? I know you were there on that day—your letter to the Church is filled with references and allusions to what Jesus said. Back then you saw Jesus as a family embarrassment. Letting people believe He's God! Saying all sorts of things guaranteed to stir up problems. Who does He think He is?

You said some pretty hateful things to Him between the time He gave the Sermon on the Mount and The Great Commission. You turned your back and wished Him dead. Oh, you didn't come right out and say it. You phrased it as only a brother can, like a verbal paper cut that stings but doesn't bleed all that much, "Leave here and go into Judea . . . no one does anything in secret when he himself seeks to be known publicly." (John 7:3-4)

And Jesus didn't miss your underlying message, did He? "My time is not yet here, but your time is always opportune." (John 7:6)

Well, your opportune time is now here.

Turn around James—your brother is here. You have a central role to play from this point forward. (Acts 12:17; 15:13; 21:18)

You both have been waiting a long time for this. And it won't be the words that carry the conversation. It will be the hugs and tears and the knowing that the big brother you've always wanted is right here. All is forgiven. Time to step into His embrace and let go of everything that has kept you apart.

Dear Elder Brother,

I know something of James' anger and embarrassment. I am often ashamed to be associated with the antics of my spiritual brothers and sisters. But You aren't troubled by what others think or whether someone else's reputation might tarnish Your own. If I give You my reputation, this won't be such a problem, will it?

True.

DAY

43

MANY OTHER THINGS

And there are also many other things which Jesus did, which if they were written in detail, I suppose that even the world itself would not contain the books that would be written.

John 21:25

Jesus, I feel a familiar sadness in my soul. Pentecost is fast approaching, and You are wrapping up Your time on earth. We won't be able to walk down a dirt road with You or share a meal much longer. You will soon hand us over to Your Spirit, and life will change.

I know, You said it was to our advantage that the Comforter come (John 16:7). But right now, it doesn't feel that way. I find it far more difficult to say goodbye and stay, than to say goodbye and leave. You're leaving and I'm staying.

Perhaps that's why You've planned one more road trip from the familiar hills of Galilee back to Jerusalem (Luke 24:49-51). The retreat is over, Your Great Commission given, and now it's time for a final goodbye and the beginning of the Church Age.

I used to read "many other things" and think of Your creative work before the world began or what You are doing in Heaven to prepare a place of us. But now I'm not so sure.

John was an old man when he penned those words—I wonder if he was thinking about those early years of Your Kingdom's expansion on earth. If that's so, then perhaps my melancholy is misplaced. You never really left at all. You're here in a different way, moving among Your children, crafting a tale so big and so wonderful that even the Internet could not access or contain a fraction of it!

Who knows when You might decide to suddenly appear, just in the nick of time to add another page to Your story!

Jesus,

You are still writing Your story across the pages of our world, and the ink splashes over into Eternity. But in some mysterious way You see to it that we each write a page or two ourselves. Every one of us is a scribe and a sinner.

Jesus, please edit my words, the grammar of my life is always in need of Your correction and comment.

Amen

DAY

44

BETHANY BLESSING

I am sending forth the promise of My Father upon you; but you are to stay in the city until you are clothed with power from on high." And He led them out as far as Bethany, and He lifted up His hands and blessed them. And it came about that while He was blessing them, He parted from them.

Luke 24:49-51

You brought them back from Galilee and told them to wait in Jerusalem for what the Father would do next. It always comes back to the Father, doesn't it?

The very first thing the Father did when He created us was to bless us (Genesis 1:28). And now the very last thing You will do in these 40 days is to bless us.

Wonder what You said?

"I'm proud of you."

"Everything is going to turn out great."

"Your life matters."

"You'll have everything you need."

"I'll be waiting."

"I'll miss you."

"I love you."

At the end of the day these are the words my heart longs to hear. To know I'm known, that I'm loved, that I matter, that I'm missed, and that there's a place for me no matter what.

Is that why You chose Bethany for Your final goodbyes?

You began Your ministry in Bethany (John 1:28-29); You came here the night before You decided to drive the moneychangers out of the Temple (Mark 11:11-19); You raised Lazarus from the dead in Bethany (John 11:1-44); and this is where Your body was anointed for burial a week before Your crucifixion (Mark 14:3).

Bethany has been the staging ground for so many things, but it is also Your home away from home. The little village of Bethany, near the Mount of Olives and close to Jerusalem, is the perfect place—it is full of good memories, a tangible reminder that Your blessings have always been wrapped around us.

Father,

Your blessings are not just a future promise, but a present reality. I will let Your blessing define me and direct me past, present and future. And I will wait with the others for the Your promise of another Comforter.

Amen.

DAY

❧ 45 ❧

OUT OF SIGHT FOR THE MOMENT

And after He had said these things, He was lifted up while they were looking on, and a cloud received Him out of their sight. And as they were gazing intently into the sky while He was going, behold, two men in white clothing stood beside them. They also said, "Men of Galilee, why do you stand looking into the sky? This Jesus, who has been taken up from you into heaven, will come in just the same way as you have watched Him go into heaven."

Acts 1:9-11

One final miracle to ponder—You can fly! And since we will have bodies like Yours (Philippians 3:20-21), does that mean we will be able to soar too? I hope so!

But Your ability to defy gravity is hardly the point. Why assign two angels to refocus Your followers' upward gaze? Are You reminding them that the story isn't over, just because the visible Author has left the building? Maybe, but there's more, isn't there?

The world propagates a storyline full of hopeless conditions and circumstances and contemplates an active or passive death in response. But You send Your angels to remind us that life is never hopeless. We've been rescued once, will be again, and it could happen at any time. There are no hopeless situations!

Father,

Remind me, the next time circumstances would suggest otherwise, that You have placed me in a happy-ending story, where hope is my birthright.

Amen

DAY

46

IN THE TEMPLE

And they, after worshiping Him, returned to Jerusalem with great joy, and were continually in the temple praising God.

Luke 24:52-53

For 40 days it seems You took them back to the key places where everything happened. Everywhere except the Temple. You seem to have steered clear of this one spot.

Why?

This place is full of Your story! You were dedicated here when You were eight days old (Luke 2:22). Simeon and Anna prophesied over You that day (Luke 2:25ff). You taught here. Healed here. Debated the religious leaders here. It isn't a stretch to say that the Temple was the center of Your operations when You were in Jerusalem.

It wasn't all that long ago You cleaned house here, turning over tables and driving out the moneychangers (Luke 19:45). But at Your death, the Temple changed forever. The veil in the Holy of holies was torn in two (Luke 23:45), making earthly intermediaries a thing of the past. You are now the only High Priest (Hebrews 3:1).

You care deeply about Your house, and so do Your children. This is where they decide to come to celebrate after You return to Heaven with a weeklong house party— right out in front of the old-order religious establishment!

But the temple isn't big enough for what is about to take place. The new wine You've been pouring into Your followers is about to burst forth, and old temple thinking doesn't have a category for this.

What You told Nicodemus on that night long ago is gathering force, "The wind blows where it wishes" (John 3:8) and the wind of Heaven is about to blow this house down (Acts 2:2)! And when Your Spirit descends upon Your children, it won't be in the temple. It will be in a home, a private place.

The time for this "temple-made-with-human-hands" has passed. A new temple has been prepared. From the day of Pentecost until the day of Your return, we will be Your temple!

Child,

Do you not know that you are a temple of God and that the Spirit of God dwells in you? (I Corinthians 3:16)

Yes! But this is an overwhelming concept I can't begin to wrap my head around.

Yes, I know.

DAY

47

A PREGNANT MOMENT
IN THE UPPER ROOM

*But you shall receive power when the Holy
Spirit has come upon you; . . . Then they
returned to Jerusalem from the mount called
Olivet, which is near Jerusalem, a Sabbath
day's journey away. When they had entered the
city, they went up to the upper room where
they were staying . . . These all with one mind
were continually devoting themselves to prayer,
along with the women, and Mary the mother
of Jesus, and with His brothers.*

Acts 1:8, 12-14

Mary! I've wanted to have this conversation with you for the
longest time. You are the only one with experience in this
sort of thing. You carried the Second Member of the Trinity
in your body for nine months.

What did the angel say to you, thirty some years and nine
months earlier? Oh yes, "The Holy Spirit will come upon

you, and the power of the Most High will overshadow you (Luke 1:35)."

Every Christmas we celebrate the end of your pregnancy with the birth of your Son and God's. Very soon we celebrate the birth of the Church and the beginning of our own "pregnancy." From now on Jesus' earthly family will be inhabited by the Third Member of the Trinity.

That is a very disturbing thought!

What was it like, being pregnant with God? When did you begin to feel the difference? Did you wonder if anyone else would notice? Did it frighten you? Were you concerned about how this profound change in you would affect those around you? Did it hurt?

It is an awesome, exhilarating, and frightening thing to consider the Holy Spirit coming upon *me*. Mary, did you teach spiritual breathing exercises to the disciples during those days of waiting?

Okay, I'll stop asking questions and listen.

You are not the first to ask me what it was like to be a vessel for God's Son. Luke interviewed me for his gospel and recorded our conversation in the first chapter of his book (Luke 1:26–56). I ran the gamut of emotion from fear and confusion (Luke 1:30,34), to surrender and joy (Luke 1:38, 47). I became a poet and a singer (Luke 1:46–55). I was swept up in the grand design of God's plan for all times (Luke 1:50–55). I was so humbled yet exhilarated that I got to be a part of the story (Luke 1:39).

This sounds a lot like what's about to happen to those filled with the Holy Spirit on that first Pentecost!

You are starting to understand.

Spirit,

Fill me too.

Amen

PROPHECY, PRAXIS,[11] AND PRAYER (BUT MAYBE NOT DRAWING LOTS)

At this time Peter stood up in the midst of the brethren (a gathering of about one hundred and twenty persons was there together), and said, "Brethren, the Scripture had to be fulfilled, which the Holy Spirit foretold by the mouth of David concerning Judas, who became a guide to those who arrested Jesus. . . . Therefore it is necessary that of the men who have accompanied us all the time that the Lord Jesus went in and out among us . . . One of these must become a witness with us of His resurrection." And they drew lots for them, and the lot fell to Matthias; and he was added to the eleven apostles.

Acts 1:15–22, 26

---

[11] The practical application and wisdom that comes from living out of what you have learned or experienced.

They are still in the Upper Room, somewhere in the Old City, with the marching orders of the Great Commission still fresh on their minds. One of their number has fallen and needs to be replaced. The traitor Judas certainly *fell* both literally and spiritually, just as David prophesied a thousand years earlier in Psalm 69:25 and Psalm109:8.

Peter, you're feeling dangerous in a good way, aren't you? You're seeing connections in the story that you missed before! All of you are. Jesus did indeed *open your minds to the Scriptures* (Luke 24:45). The first sermon you will be giving in a day or two will be full of Old Testament prophecies and connections to Jesus' life, death and resurrection (Acts 2:14-36). Powerful and dangerous stuff! Your message will pierce the hearts and souls of 3,000 on that day (Acts 2:37,41).

But we're not there yet. We're still in the in-between time. The Spirit has been promised but the fulfillment of that promise has yet to happen.

Today, we're going through the exercise of selecting a replacement for Judas. Everyone rightly assumes that more witnesses to Jesus' resurrection will be needed.

I have no idea how successful you were in your selection of Matthias (Acts 1:26)—he is never mentioned again. A few years down the road, Jesus will call Paul to be His disciple (Acts 9) and the fruitfulness of that choice is obvious.

However, the way you all go about discerning God's will (on your maiden voyage into this new *openness* to understanding of His Word) is very instructive. You search the Scriptures for guidance, you value the wisdom of practical experience or *praxis* (Acts 1:23), and you pray (Acts 1:24). Is there a more powerful combination for finding God's will, or opening *our* minds to the Scriptures? I don't think so.

This threefold approach, to discerning Your will, will be the gold standard from now on.

But what about the *drawing lots* business? It certainly was a popular approach in the Old Testament; there are dozens and dozens of examples where it actually worked and was encouraged by You!

Lots are cast by the High Priest in Leviticus 16:8 to determine which goat will be the sin offering; in Joshua 7:14, lots are used to discover the traitor in their midst; and in Jonah 1:7, the lot falls on Jonah as the source of their calamity. Just to name a few.

But the selection of Matthias, as the twelfth disciple, is the last time lots are ever mentioned in Scripture. Seems that after Your Spirit is poured out on Your followers, lots loose their efficacy. Things are definitely changing!

Dear Wisdom of the Ages,

There isn't anything more important than discerning Your will, and having the courage and heart to do it! Open my mind to Your Word, tune my heart to Your Spirit, and live out Your will in and through my life.

Amen

DAY

❧{ 49 }❧

NO MORE DYING IN
THE WILDERNESS

*But God raised Him from the dead; and for
many days He appeared to those who came up
with Him from Galilee to Jerusalem, the very
ones who are now His witnesses to the people.*

Acts 13:30–31

For 40 days You stayed with us.

Ate with us.

Walked with us.

Talked with us in groups and individually.

Took us back to where it all began.

I understand that You wanted us to know beyond a shadow
of a doubt that You rose from the dead. You are exactly who
You said You were—God the Son.

But it seems that there is more behind these 40 days. You're intentionally changing something within those with whom You're spending time.

You're weaning them from Your physical presence.

Transitioning them to life in the Spirit.

Giving them their marching orders.

Saying goodbye.

And one thing more.

You want them to never lose the wonder of what they experienced.

You've taken them back through the story to the very places where it took place. Reminded them that it really happened. Explained what they missed or mistook. Settled once and for all the grand narrative of Your redemptive mission. And then You took the time (40 days' worth) to see to it that they're own stories were woven into the very fabric of Your story.

This time the life-changing moment will be just that— life changing! Promises and vows won't dissipate with the morning dew. This time the desert won't dampen the wonder of their deliverance. These 40 days will replace 40 years of wandering in the wilderness (Deuteronomy 1). This time the first generation of believers won't have to die off before they go into the Land. This time the story will stick.

It worked! The first fruits of Your Church kept the faith, followed through, even unto their own deaths—because they knew that even death was not the end of the story. And they never forgot the exquisitely painful, piercingly wonderful joy of Your risen presence in and through and around and beyond their lives.

Father,

We are undone and made over. Forever. Thank You for taking this time to make it perfectly clear. Thank You for making room for us in Your story.

Amen

DAY

50

PENTECOST

When the day of Pentecost had come, they were all together in one place. And suddenly there came from heaven a noise like a violent rushing wind, and it filled the whole house where they were sitting. And there appeared to them tongues as of fire distributing themselves, and they rested on each one of them. And they were all filled with the Holy Spirit.

Acts 2:1–4

Happy Birthday, Church! Happy Birthday, Bride of Christ! Old things have passed away! New things have come!

God's family is finding its voice.

And if Christ should choose to return on the 2,000th anniversary of the Church (and He just might), we only have a handful of years left.

And this is the Good News! You don't have to wait for eternity to experience Heaven—the Kingdom of God is not only among us—it is in us!

And on that day, so long ago, the Church was birthed and the Spirit given. And they took to the streets and crowed! The exquisitely-painful, piercingly-wonderful joy they experienced on that long-ago day is still as sweet, and fresh, and clear as it ever was! And what's more -

Everything is speeding up. Aslan is on the move!

What used to take a year, now unfolds in a month. What used to take a month, now needs less than a day.

Once again, the clarion call is given. I can almost hear the trumpet sound. The time for heroes is at hand. We need to find our voices. And maybe, just maybe, learn a thing or two about crowing.

Ah Daddy!

The last time a cock crowed, it was to announce Peter's threefold denial of his Lord. But before Peter's broken promise and crushing disappointment, You tied the rooster's crowing to Your Second Coming[12] (Mark 13:35). Oh to be fully awake and at my post on that day; to add my own, full-throated crow to the chorus of those who will celebrate the return of the King at the end of days!

And who knows how soon that day may be?

Only You.

---

[12] "Therefore, be on the alert--for you do not know when the master of the house is coming, whether in the evening, at midnight, or when the rooster crows, or in the morning--." (Mark 13:35)

A Few Words about
Lectio Divina

Athanasius thought spiritual progress unlikely without it.

St. Benedict made it a regular part of each day.

Dom Guigo II saw it as a ladder to Heaven.

Ignatius of Loyola discovered it while convalescing after a cannon ball broke his leg.

It makes some uncomfortable. Others avoid it altogether. Many have no idea what it is. And some have tasted this ancient discipline and found it to be sweet nectar for their souls. It is *lectio divina* (spiritual reading as it is often called).

Lectio divina invites the Third Member of the Trinity to awaken the imagination of our hearts, illumine the text and usher us inside the biblical narrative. Most of my training was focused on the outside of the biblical text—observation, interpretation, application, and correlation. Discover the historical context, mix in the grammatical syntax of the original languages, parse and pray.

That is well and good. Christianity is the thinking man or woman's faith. Name another religion that invites you to question your faith—bet you can't. Jesus' three favorite questions are, "Have you not heard?" "Have you not read?" "Do you not know?" Jesus saw faith and reason as fast friends. But faith and reason are not the same thing. Faith travels further than reason. Where sight fails, faith endures.

For over 30 years I've had the privilege of inviting students into the world of Peter, James, and John. We've argued the authorship of Hebrews, compared and contrasted the Gospels, and traveled with Paul on his missionary journeys. I even wrote a book on the New Testament (*The Garimus File*).

In many ways the New Testament is a comfortable, familiar book for me. However, words like "comfortable" and "familiar" will never do justice to anyone's encounter with the living God. And if they do, then all is not well and good.

Lectio divina seeks to encounter the Author of the text. And when you do, those moments may well be couched in a "piercingly painful, impossibly wonderful joy."

Take John Chapter 14, for example. In the chapter leading up to this, Jesus washes the disciples' feet; Judas abandons the group to pursue his mission of betrayal; and Peter is told by Jesus that his boast to follow Him even to death will dissipate with the coming dawn. Confusion and fear abound. And then Chapter 14 opens with Jesus' words, "Let not your heart be troubled."

Jesus is saying goodbye. The cross waits. The darkness before the dawn will be overwhelming. Yet, in the midst of all this, everyone seems to have a question.

Thomas wants to know the way. "I am the way," replies Jesus. Philip just wants to see the Father. "He who has seen Me has seen the Father," answers Jesus. And Thaddeus (in my opinion) voices the general confusion they all have about what is happening.

I've read and taught this passage dozens of times. It is almost funny, the way they keep interrupting Jesus. Yet each interruption opens the door to another profound truth. All of this a person can glean by simply observing the text.

It was only when I stepped into the story, and put my elbows on the table with the rest of the disciples, that the Author of the text found me out. I was soaking in the atmosphere, looking around at the faces of the disciples as they tried to understand Jesus' words. My imagination was filling in where the text was silent.

I see we have another guest at the table this evening!

Jesus' words scared me. I felt like a party crasher. I've always studied this event like a white-coated technician looking on. But now I was no longer an outside observer but part of their story!

It seems that everyone has a question for Me tonight. Then He looked directly at me, *Would you like to ask Me a question?*

I just wanted to crawl under the table. I'm not supposed to be part of the story. This is way too personal. I have no words. This isn't how I've ever come to this passage.

Gary, I know the question that's on your heart. I've always known. Here's My answer, 'No—I will not leave you orphaned.'

I cannot write these words without tears even now. I became fatherless at thirteen and His words touch a tender, broken part of my heart that is always with me. In that moment, when Jesus questioned me, He drove that truth much deeper into my soul than it has ever been before. I've known the truth of Jesus' promise for a long time—in my head. But carrying it around in my head was like carrying a prescription in my pocket and never putting it in my mouth and swallowing it.

That day I swallowed.

It just so happens that the words I "heard" Jesus speak are recorded in verse 18 of that very chapter. From the outside of the story, I could only "read" them: they were written for everyone. But that day Jesus "spoke" them just to me.

Is it possible that I smuggled in some self-talk, old family rules, a bit of the world, and even entertained a word or two from the Enemy of our souls as I practiced *lectio divina* that day? Yes! And I've found myself in similar peril while "objectively" studying God Word with all the linguistic, cultural, and hermeneutical tools I have at my disposal.

The thing is, four chapters earlier Jesus said, "My sheep hear My voice." (John 10:27) You don't have to be a great exegete to discern that God has a voice; He uses it, and His children can hear it. A few chapters before that, at the height of His popularity, He told a group of Jewish scholars who opposed Him, "You search the Scriptures, because you think that in them you have eternal life; and it is these that bear witness of Me; and you are unwilling to come to Me, that you may have life" (John 5:39-40).

The Truth was standing right in front of them. They had studied the Scriptures for most of their lives. But all of their accumulated knowledge was blocking them from the real hope of eternal life.

I've lived in a world where the cure to just about everything is found in more knowledge. I don't live there any more (at least I try not to live there). Eternal life is personal not propositional.

So, I invite you to "come to the Savior." When you read the Scriptures with that desire in your heart, you are very close to the practice of *lectio divina*.

How The Story from Easter to Pentecost Fits Together

Easter Sunday Morning

Mary Magdalene, Mary the mother of James, Salome, Joanna, and at least one other woman make their way to the tomb before sunrise, planning to finish the preparations for Jesus' body that were postponed due to Sabbath restrictions. (Matthew 28:1; Mark 16:1-2; Luke 24:1,10; John 20:1)

An angel descends from heaven causing an earthquake as he rolls back the stone that covered the entrance to the tomb. He then sits on the stone and waits with a second angel. (Matthew 28:2; Mark 16:5-7; Luke 24:4-7; John 20:12)

The guards, who were tasked with guarding the tomb, flee the angel in terror. (Matthew 28:4)

The women arrive at the empty tomb at daybreak. (Matthew 28:5).

Apparently Mary Magdalene runs back to find Peter and John, before hearing what the angel has to say. She tells Peter and John (who are probably not with the other disciples), "They have taken the Lord out of the tomb, and we do not know where they have laid him." (John 20:2)

The rest of the women listen to the angel who tells them that Jesus isn't there, that He has risen, and that they should go tell the disciples to go to Galilee where Jesus will meet them. (Matthew 28:5; Luke 24:22-24)

While the women are on their way back to the city, Jesus greets them and repeats the angel's instructions. (Matthew 28:6, 9-10; John 20:11-17)

While all of this is going on, some of the guards run back to town to report to the chief priests what has happened. (Matthew 28:11)

John and Peter run to the tomb to verify Mary's report (John 20:3-6) and find the tomb empty. John sees the face cloth, which had been on Jesus' head, folded up in a place by it, and believed that more was going on than had been reported (John 20:8-9), and then Peter and John go back home. (John 20:10)

Mary Magdalene (likely following Peter and John) returns to the tomb and is the first to actually see Jesus (Mark 16:9). Mary mistakes Him for the gardener until Jesus calls her by name (John 20:15-16) and says to her, "Stop clinging to Me, for I have not yet ascended to the Father." (John 20:17)

The chief priests assemble the elders and bribe the guards to say that Jesus' disciples stole the body. They promise to protect the guards from any reprisal by the governor. (Matthew 28:12-15)

The women find the other disciples (perhaps in Bethany) minus Peter and John and tell them what they have seen and heard. Some believe, but some doubt. (Luke 24:10-11)

An Afternoon Road Trip to Emmaus

Clopas and his friend learn of the report from the women and take off for the town of Emmaus, about seven miles from Jerusalem. They meet Jesus along the way but don't recognize Him (Luke 24:13-24). Jesus explains that all scripture is about Him (Luke 24:25-27). They invite Jesus to stay for dinner, and when He blesses the bread, they recognize Him and He vanishes from sight. (Luke 24:28-32; Mark 16:12)

Some time during the day, Jesus appears privately to Peter. (I Corinthians 15:5)

Jesus' First Appearance to the Disciples

Cleopas and his buddy decide to return to Jerusalem to tell the disciples what happened (Luke 24:33-35). While they are sharing their story, Jesus appears in their midst and invites them to touch Him, and even eats a piece of fish to prove that He isn't a ghost. He opens their minds to understand the Scriptures and the implication for the entire world. (Luke 24:36-49; John 20:19-23)

Thomas is not with the other disciples when Jesus first appears to them and refuses to believe that Jesus has really risen from the dead. "Unless I see in His hands the mark of the nails," vows Thomas, "and place my finger into the mark of the nails, and place my hand into His side, I will never believe." (John 20:24-25)

Jesus' Second Appearance to the Disciples Eight Days Later

Jesus appears to Thomas and the rest of the disciples, and Thomas believes, "My Lord and my God!"(John 20:26-29)

A Long Road Trip to Galilee

The eleven disciples travel from Jerusalem to Galilee to meet Jesus on the mountain. (Matthew 28:16)

Jesus' Third Appearance to the Disciples

Peter and six other disciples decide to go fishing at the Sea of Tiberias which is located on the lower west side of Sea of Galilee. This is also the location where Jesus fed the five thousand (John 6:1-14) and where He started walking across the water to meet up with His disciples (John 6:16-21). No wonder they were drawn to this location! They fish all night but catch nothing; a stranger on shore tells them to cast their nets on the right side of the boat; they cannot pull in the enormous catch; Peter recognizes that it is Jesus on the shore. (John 21:1-14)

On the Mountain in Galilee

The disciples are joined (in my opinion) by more than 500 other believers on the mountain in Galilee (I Corinthians 15:6). Jesus gives them the Great Commission, telling them to go and make disciples of all nations, promising to always be with them. (Matthew 28:18-20).

After Jesus' commission to the 500, He meets with His little half-brother James. (I Corinthians 15:7)

Back to Jerusalem

Jesus tells them to stay in Jerusalem until the Holy Spirit had come. (Acts 1:3-8).

Last Road Trip from Jerusalem to Bethany

Jesus leads them from Jerusalem to Bethany to say goodbye. (Luke 24: 50-53; Mark 16:19; Acts 1:9-12)

Pentecost Sunday

On Pentecost they gather in one place and the Holy Spirit comes with signs and wonders. (Acts 2:1-13)

Peter preaches his first sermon and 3000 believe. (Acts 2:14-41)

Note: Many have attempted to reconcile all of the biblical accounts from Easter to Pentecost. Here are three sites I found useful –

https://answersingenesis.org/jesus-christ/resurrection/christs-
resurrection-four-accounts-one-reality/

https://www.compellingtruth.org/resurrection-accounts.html

http://www.apologeticspress.org/apcontent.aspx?category=6&article=730

Gary Stanley is a short story author, mentor and curriculum writer with a PhD in Communication. He partners with people who desire to live redemptively in hostile and stressful environments through teaching, speaking and writing.

Go to Amazon.com for other books by Gary Stanley, such as *What My Dog Has Taught Me About Life* and *How to Make a Moose Run . . . and Other Great Things my Dad Taught Me.*

Gary can be reached at garystanley@me.com.

Made in the USA
Columbia, SC
11 June 2021